Home Office Research Study 250

Programmes for black and Asian offenders on probation: Lessons for developing practice

Beverly Powis and Rachel K. Walmsley
Offenders and Corrections Unit
Home Office Research, Development and Statistics

The views expressed in this report are those of the authors, not necessarily those of the Home Office (nor do they reflect Government policy).

Home Office Research, Development and Statistics Directorate
October 2002

Home Office Research Studies

The Home Office Research Studies are reports on research undertaken by or on behalf of the Home Office. They cover the range of subjects for which the Home Secretary has responsibility. Other publications produced by the Research, Development and Statistics Directorate include Findings, Statistical Bulletins and Statistical Papers.

The Research, Development and Statistics Directorate

RDS is part of the Home Office. The Home Office's purpose is to build a safe, just and tolerant society in which the rights and responsibilities of individuals, families and communities are properly balanced and the protection and security of the public are maintained.

RDS is also part of National Statistics (NS). One of the aims of NS is to inform Parliament and the citizen about the state of the nation and provide a window on the work and performance of government, allowing the impact of government policies and actions to be assessed.

Therefore –

Research Development and Statistics Directorate exists to improve policy making, decision taking and practice in support of the Home Office purpose and aims, to provide the public and Parliament with information necessary for informed debate and to publish information for future use.

First published 2002
Application for reproduction should be made to the Communication Development Unit, Room 201, Home Office, 50 Queen Anne's Gate, London SW1H 9AT.
© Crown copyright 2002   ISBN   1 84082 878 1
                           ISSN   0072 6435

Foreword

The Home Office has been reviewing the effectiveness of interventions with offenders under probation supervision in England and Wales as part of the Government's Crime Reduction Programme. The study on which this report is based was conducted to inform the development of probation work with black and Asian offenders.

The report includes the findings of a survey of previous, current and planned Probation Service provision specifically targeting black and Asian offenders conducted in June 2000. This found that 13 programmes had been developed in ten Services, 5 of which were still running. Ten of these group-work programmes were studied in detail to identify the factors that those developing, delivering or, in some cases, managing the programmes believed contributed to their success or failure.

It provides a useful summary of what is known about working with black and Asian offenders on probation which has informed the development of new programmes to be piloted in selected probation areas. Further research has also been commissioned to increase our knowledge about the needs and experiences of black and Asian offenders on probation.

Chris Lewis
Head of Offenders and Corrections Unit
Research, Development and Statistics Directorate

Acknowledgements

We would like to thank all the probation staff who contributed to this study through taking part in interviews and responding to questionnaires. We would also like to thank all those who participated in the research Reference Group and Steering Group for their valuable help with the project.

We are grateful to Sarah Pepper, Coretta Phillips, Claire Flood-Page and Nicola Parry of the Home Office Research, Development and Statistics Directorate for their input into this research.

Finally, we would like to thank Dr Ben Bowling of Kings College, London who acted as an external reviewer. Thanks also to Professor Clive Hollin of the University of Leicester for his advice on conducting the research.

Beverly Powis
Rachel K. Walmsley

Contents

Summary

The Home Office has been reviewing the effectiveness of community-based interventions with offenders under probation supervision in England and Wales as part of the Government's Crime Reduction Programme. In 1999 Probation Services were invited to submit proposals to develop effective programmes for particular groups of offenders or offences (including sex offenders, substance misusers, drink-drivers, violent offenders and domestic violence offenders). Proposals for specialist projects such as those for black and Asian offenders were also invited. However, while the importance of developing interventions for black and Asian offenders was recognised because of their over-representation in the criminal justice system, the lack of knowledge about effective practice made it impossible to develop new interventions for them. The study on which this report is based was commissioned to identify what is known about the criminogenic needs[1] of black and Asian offenders, the probation provision currently available and effective approaches to reducing their reoffending.

Existing evidence

The Probation Service deals with more black and fewer Asian offenders than would be expected from their distribution in the general population. As little research has examined the criminogenic factors associated with their offending, it is difficult to conclude if black and Asian offenders have unique criminogenic needs. However, it is known that some minority ethnic groups have higher levels of educational underachievement and unemployment that may place them at greater risk of reoffending as these are factors associated with high levels of offending. It is possible that combined effects of the relative deprivation of their communities, educational underachievement, unemployment and institutional racism means that they are both less able to achieve their goals through legitimate means and are more likely to experience one or more factors that puts them at risk of offending.

It is also difficult to draw any firm conclusions from the literature as to whether separate provision should be available for black and Asian offenders. There are arguments that support running separate programmes for this group of offenders but also those that advocate mixed group-work provision. There is, as yet, little empirical evidence to substantiate either position. However, research does show that groups with only a small

---

1. Criminogenic needs are those factors that contribute directly to criminal behaviour, such as anti-social attitudes, drug dependency or limited cognitive skills (Vennard et al., 1997).

proportion of black and Asian offenders attending are unlikely to be effective in addressing their needs because of feelings of isolation and disconnection with the rest of the group.

This study

In June 2000, a survey of Probation Services in England and Wales[2] was undertaken to identify the extent and nature of previous, current and planned provision for black and Asian offenders. Forty-five of the 54 Services in existence at the time of the survey replied (a response rate of 83%). In-depth interviews with staff involved in the development, delivery and, in some cases, management of ten of the programmes were also conducted. Any evaluations that had been conducted on programmes were examined. The aim was to identify any evidence from practice that would indicate that certain approaches are more effective in reducing offending behaviour amongst such offenders and to examine the factors that lead to the successful implementation and delivery of interventions to this offender group. The study was limited in that the views of offenders were not sought and interviews were conducted with management in very few services.

The scale and nature of probation group-work programmes for black and Asian offenders

The survey identified 13 programmes that had been developed in ten services specifically to target black and Asian offenders. Five of these were running at the time of the survey, the remainder being no longer offered to offenders. Ten services reported that they intended to provide an intervention for black and Asian offenders in the near future.

Four distinct types of programme were identified. These were:

1. Black Empowerment Groups (three of ten);
2. Black Empowerment within General Offending Programmes (four of ten);
3. Black Empowerment and Reintegration Programmes (one of ten); and
4. Offence Specific Programmes (two of ten)

Programmes tended to be based on a range of theoretical models, but all used cognitive-behavioural approaches. Most (seven of ten) groups were only available to men. While the others were open to female participants, in practice they mainly received referrals for men.

---

2. The National Probation Service for England and Wales was formed on 1 April 2001 and replaced the 54 Probation Services. It comprises of a National Directorate and 42 Local Probation Boards.

Group participants were from a wide age range and a diversity of ethnic backgrounds. Opinions were divided among the staff interviewed as to the benefits of having a diversity of ethnic backgrounds in a single group. Some staff saw this as beneficial as it raised awareness of cultural diversity; others thought it was detrimental to offenders and further marginalised those in the minority. This was especially so for Asian offenders who tended to be in the minority in most groups designed for black and Asian offenders.

The effectiveness of programmes

All staff interviewed were committed to running the programmes and felt that they were effective in reducing offending amongst black and Asian offenders. Only four of the programmes had been formally evaluated and two have conducted a reconviction analysis. No studies had considered the cost-effectiveness of the programmes. However, although it is difficult to draw firm conclusions because of small sample sizes, the results of these evaluations were encouraging. For example, the evaluations of both the *Black Offending Behaviour Programme* run by Greater Manchester Probation Service and Inner London Probation Service's *Black Self-Development and Educational Attainment Group* (Durrance *et al.*, 2001) had very positive feedback from both staff and offenders involved in the programme. Psychometric test scores showed changes in a positive direction after completing Greater Manchester's *Black Offending Behaviour Programme* (Williams, 2001). No reconviction analyses had been conducted on either of these programmes because they had not been running for a sufficient length of time at the time the research was completed.

A study of reconviction rates of those doing the *Black Self-Development Programme* run by Inner London Probation Service compared outcomes for offenders doing this programme with those for white offenders completing a similar programme. The study reported considerably lower reconviction figures for black programme completers compared to white offenders: 51 per cent (18/35) of black offenders were reconvicted within two years of completing the programme compared to 75 per cent (38/51) of white offenders (Durrance *et al.*, 2000). A reconviction study was also conducted on a small number (13) of offenders starting the West Midlands Probation Service's *Black People and Offending Programme*. This found that only 25 per cent (two of eight) were reconvicted two years after the programme although their predicted reconviction rate was 50 per cent (using OGRS2[3]). Sixty per cent (three of five) of those who did not complete the programme were reconvicted compared to a predicted rate of 48 per cent (Dunn, 2000).

3.   OGRS2 is a standard reconviction predictor that is based on factors including age, sex and criminal records from samples of offenders from all parts of England and Wales. It is used to produce predicted rates of reconviction for offenders.

Conclusion

The current study found little separate or specialist group-work provision for black and Asian offenders in probation services. Many programmes that had been set up were no longer being delivered. However, staff who were involved in developing or delivering programmes targeting black and Asian offenders felt there was a need for separate, specialist provision and that such programmes were effective in reducing reoffending amongst this offender group. However, because there is so little research in this area to date, it is not possible to provide empirical evidence to either support or refute this belief.

Factors that were considered by programme developers and deliverers to be important in the success of programmes are listed below. It should be noted that many of these factors are not unique to working with black and Asian offenders but can be applied to all offending behaviour programmes:

- full service commitment to running the programme;
- good management support of programmes with the provision of adequate resources and work-load relief to develop programmes and adequate training for staff to deliver programmes;
- a good facilitator who is understanding of the needs of this client group and is of minority ethnic background;
- using external experts to develop and evaluate programmes and to act as mentors to participants;
- incorporating a range of issues including offending behaviour, education, employment and training with sound theoretical base which may include cognitive-behavioural techniques;
- longer, more intensive programmes (although it has been noted elsewhere that the use of longer programmes may result in unequal treatment of black and Asian offenders if referral to the programme is not based on an assessment of their criminogenic need);
- an active participation learning style;
- need to introduce measures to maintain programme integrity;
- effective referral and case-management systems;
- effective targeting which recognises that only some black or Asian offenders will need separate provision; and
- thorough evaluations to examine the effectiveness of programmes.

The Home Office is currently undertaking further work to improve its understanding of the needs of black and Asian offenders on probation and the types of group-work interventions that are likely to be effective in reducing their reoffending. This work includes the commissioning of a survey of 500 black and Asian men on probation. The National Probation Service is also piloting five different models of working with black and Asian offenders in selected probation areas. The models will be evaluated. The results of these two studies, together with this report, will form an evidence base on which future work with black and Asian offenders on probation can build.

1.   Introduction

The Home Office has been reviewing the effectiveness of community-based interventions with offenders under probation supervision in England and Wales as part of the Government's Crime Reduction Programme. In 1999 Probation Services were invited to submit proposals to develop effective programmes to target a wide range of offenders including sex offenders, substance misusers, drink-drivers, violent offenders and domestic violence offenders. Proposals for specialist projects such as those for black and Asian offenders were also invited. Programmes had to meet a number of criteria before they were awarded 'Pathfinder status'. These included being based on a recognised model of change and having a strong evidence base that the intervention could reduce participants' offending behaviour. Pathfinder programmes are currently being developed to an 'accreditable' standard. Once a programme has been accredited by the Joint Prisons and Probation Accreditation Panel, it will be 'rolled out' on a national basis.

However, it was not possible to develop a Pathfinder programme for black and Asian offenders at that time, despite their being a key group of interest to the Home Office, because there was felt to be insufficient knowledge about effective probation work with them. This study was commissioned to fill this knowledge gap. It draws upon three sources of information:

1. A literature review of published research to establish any criminogenic factors associated with the offending behaviour of black and Asian offenders in particular, and to review research on approaches to reducing reoffending by black and Asian offenders. It was hoped to consider the cost-effectiveness of such approaches, but no studies that did this were found;

2. A survey of all 54 Probation Services in England and Wales to identify current, planned and previous provision for black and Asian offenders on probation and combination orders[4] within Probation Services; and

3. Case studies of ten programmes for black and Asian offenders identified in the survey.

---

4.   The terms given to community sentences changed in April 2001. Probation orders are now called community rehabilitation orders, community service orders are now community punishment orders and combination orders are now community punishment and rehabilitation orders.

Definitional issues

The ethnic monitoring system used by Probation Services at the time of this study asked offenders to tick a box (Black, White, Other (please specify) or Refused). They also answered the question, 'Where would you say your ethnic group comes from?' and selected from the list of countries provided[5]. However, even with this limited coding system, Probation Services had a significant proportion of ethnic data missing, especially in recent years (Home Office, 2001; HMIP, 2000).

For this study, it was decided to use the terms 'black' and 'Asian' as they are used in the 1991 Census of Population. 'Black' is defined as African, Caribbean or Other. 'Asian' is defined as Bangladeshi, Indian, Pakistani or Other (but does not include people of Chinese origin). These were chosen because at that time they were used by the Prison Service and by general population surveys such as the Labour Force Survey. This makes it easier to compare findings of this study with data from other relevant sources. In this report 'black' is written as such, in line with Home Office race equality guidelines. However, it should be noted that there was some disagreement about this among members of the project's reference group[6], some of whom wished 'black' to be written with a capital B.

The literature on black and Asian offenders is sometimes unclear as to which ethnic group is being discussed. Terms such as 'ethnic minority' or 'black' are frequently used but not always defined. This is important for two reasons. Firstly, it makes it difficult to compare studies and, secondly, it hides very real differences between people of African, African/Caribbean, Indian, Pakistani, Bangladeshi and other Asian descent[7]. Therefore, the lack of detailed classifications of offenders' ethnic groups gives less weight to any tentative conclusions that can be drawn from some studies. Generally, research was about *male* black and Asian offenders: none of the literature reviewed differentiated between male and female offenders.

It became clear during the case study stage of this research that each probation programme used a different definition when referring to different groups of minority ethnic offenders. For example, sometimes the term 'black' included those from African/Caribbean and Asian descent, whereas at other times, the term 'black' referred only to those whose ethnic group

---

5. The National Probation Service adopted the coding frame used in the 2001 Census as the standard method of recording ethnicity for offenders and staff at the beginning of 2002.
6. A reference group, made up of practitioners from various Probation Services across England and Wales, was set up at the beginning of the study to provide advice and information.
7. This is especially important in the generic 'Asian' category because the experiences of Bangladeshis and Pakistanis are very different from those of Indians who make up the majority of this group (Flood-Page, 1999, Pathak, 2000).

came from Africa or the Caribbean. Some groups were less specific and were open to anyone who had a 'common experience of racism and discrimination'. This inconsistent use of ethnic definitions makes it more difficult to compare groups either with each other or with other groups of offenders.

Separate or specialist provision?

It also became clear in the research that it is important to differentiate between 'separate' and 'specialist' provision for black and Asian offenders. *Separate* provision is where programmes are provided in groups exclusively for black and Asian offenders. The work done in separate groups may be the same or similar to that done by white offenders. *Specialist* provision is where black and Asian offenders are offered interventions that specifically address their perceived needs where these are different for white offenders.

Structure of the report

This report examines the evidence on successful implementation and delivery of programmes to black and Asian offenders and suggests factors that are important to their success. Chapter 2 reviews the literature on explanations of offending by black and Asian offenders and examines the case for separate provision. Chapter 3 examines the scale and nature of previous and current programmes for black and Asian offenders. The evidence for their effectiveness is considered in Chapter 4. Finally, Chapter 5 draws some conclusions and sets out factors that those involved in either developing or delivering the programmes believed to be vital to the success of programmes for black and Asian offenders.

Ethnic minority offenders on probation

The most recent Probation Statistics that include ethnic monitoring data are those for 1998. Table 2.1 indicates that the Probation Service dealt with *more* black and *less* South Asian people than would be expected from their representation in the general population.

Table 2.1:   Offenders starting community sentences by ethnic group[1]

Probation	CSO	Combination	General population Order	Aged 18-54[2]
Black	4.5	5.6	5.6	2.2
South Asian	1.3	2.6	2.1	3.4
Other minority ethnic group	1.5	1.9	1.6	1.4
White	92.6	89.9	90.8	93.0

Note
1. Figures taken from Tables 7.1, 7.2. and 7.3 Probation Statistics 1998
2. Figures taken from the 1996-98 Labour Force Survey

The percentage of offenders from minority ethnic groups on probation or combination orders is similar for most offence categories. However, a significantly larger proportion of those serving a probation or combination order after being convicted for robbery were from minority ethnic groups[8]. The proportion of people serving probation or combination orders for fraud or forgery offences from minority ethnic groups was also greater than would be expected (Probation Statistics, 1998). The debate about whether this reflects elevated rates of offending or discriminatory criminal justice processing have been well rehearsed elsewhere, but are beyond the scope of this report (see for example, Smith, 1997 and Bowling and Phillips, 2002).

---

8.   Fifteen per cent of people on a probation order for robbery were black and 4.7 per cent were from other minority ethnic groups. 18.6 per cent of those doing a combination order after being convicted for robbery were black and 8.3 per cent from other minority ethnic groups (Tables 7.1. and 7.3, Probation Statistics 1998).

Explanations of offending

A question that was asked at the beginning of this study was 'do black and Asian offenders have particular criminogenic needs that programmes need to address?'. No research that identified particular criminogenic needs was found. Some researchers have, however, suggested that they may have different motivations for offending. Existing probation group-work programmes specifically for black and Asian offenders often seem to be built around the premise that these offenders' behaviour is the product of racism and that they therefore require specialist rehabilitation which focuses on empowerment and related issues (Lawrence, 1995). It is therefore important that this underlying premise is correct in order for such a programme to be successful.

A small project conducted in 1987 examined social inquiry reports[9] prepared for 25 black and 25 white offenders by 13 white probation officers and conducted interviews with the same officers. It found that, in interviews, officers gave racism as the most frequent explanation offered for black offending (Denney, 1992). Another study recorded the experiences of people in a mixed offending behaviour group in Wandsworth Prison (Fisher and Watkins, 1993). This found that, when there was a majority of black members in the group, the impact of institutionalised racism and the criminalisation of certain sections of the black population took on prominence compared with explanations rooted at the individual level.

It is, however, difficult to untangle peoples' motivation for offending, or for any other type of behaviour. One study found that offenders themselves sometimes give different explanations for their offending. A study based on interviews with 30 black offenders, 15 black and white staff and 15 representatives from local organisations and community groups found that black and Asian offenders identified financial issues or unemployment when asked what they believed to be the reasons for offending by black people (Lawrence, 1995). Representatives from community groups placed greater emphases on education, training and discrimination and probation staff emphasised discrimination, frustration or family circumstances. Similarly, interviews with 28 minority ethnic offenders by Inner London Probation Service suggested that offenders did not feel that a black empowerment group was relevant to their needs because they felt that being black had nothing to do with their offending and they did not have a problem with race (ILPS, 1996).

A study by Barker et al. (1993) suggested money and image as reasons for offending by black and Asian people. Forty-five street robbery offenders (approximately two-thirds of whom were black) were interviewed. Offenders gave money as the reason for their offending and said that they spent the money on expensive clothes, luxuries and cannabis.

---

9.   Social inquiry reports were replaced by pre-sentence reports in the mid-1990s.

It is difficult to say from the above whether the motivations for offending are different for black and Asian offenders. Motivation in the general offender population is often the need for material goods, status and excitement. People who are less able to achieve these needs through legal means, for example because they are unemployed, poor or have bad housing, are at a higher risk of offending than other groups (Farrington, 1997). However, the institutional racism that has been identified in a number of public services[10], together with the relative deprivation of their communities discussed below, means that black and Asian offenders may have less access to legitimate opportunities than their white counterparts. Therefore, it is possible that, while the direct cause of offending given by black and Asian offenders might be the same, they may be more likely to be in a disadvantaged position because of the additional difficulties they face.

Risk factors

Research has consistently identified some factors as associated with high levels of offending. These include poor school performance, truancy, school exclusion, low income, unemployment and drug use (Farrington, 1996, Farrington, 1997, Graham and Bowling, 1995, Flood-Page et al., 2000). The high levels of deprivation among ethnic minority communities place black, Pakistani and Bangladeshi offenders especially 'at risk'. For example, evidence gathered by the Department for Education and Employment in 2000 clearly shows a pattern of continuous underachievement for certain ethnic groups that starts in early education, continues through further and higher education, and persists in the labour market (Pathak, 2000). School exclusions are disproportionately high among African-Caribbean boys (Flood-Page, 1999; Commission for Racial Equality, 1996). Black, Pakistani and Bangladeshi children do less well than white children in the attainment of GCSEs and A-levels[11] (DfEE, 2001a, DfEE, 2001b). Underachievement at school may be caused by a combination of reasons including regular truancy, social class, low teacher expectations, conflict and tension with teachers and a high relative probability of being permanently excluded (Pathak, 2000). All of these factors may be influenced by racism.

Turning to employment, the white population had higher employment rates than all ethnic minority groups for both men and women in 1998/99. Pakistani and Bangladeshi men were three times as likely to be unemployed as white people (18% compared to 6%) (Sly et al., 1999). Black young men are twice as likely as white men to be unemployed and levels

---

10. See, for example, Coombe (1986), Bowling (1991), Bagihole (1997) and Bowling and Phillips (2002).
11. This is not true of all minority ethnic groups as Indian and other Asian children achieve better results than those who are white. There were also marked increases in the achievement of five or more GCSEs A*-C grades for black, Indian and other Asian young people between 1998 and 2000.

of youth unemployment are consistently higher for them than any group other than Pakistanis (Flood-Page, 1999). Bangladeshis and Pakistanis are the poorest communities in the UK, with 60 per cent living in low-income households (Pathak, 2000). Bangladeshi and African-Caribbean heads of household are also most likely to be in social housing (DETR, 2000).

On this basis it is difficult to establish if African/Caribbean, Asian and white people do offend for the same or different reasons. However, it is likely that the relative deprivation of the ethnic minority communities and the impact of institutional racism means that black and Asian people may find it more difficult to achieve their goals legitimately and be more likely to experience one or more of the factors associated with a greater risk of offending. This suggests that probation work needs to take account of the problems that black and Asian people suffer disproportionately (Bowling and Phillips, 2002) and that programmes may need to focus on more than simply empowerment issues.

Do black and Asian offenders benefit from separate provision?

Another issue that is important for developing probation work is whether black and Asian offenders would benefit from separate provision. Researchers' views on this differ.

Arguments for separate provision

Some research has addressed the issue of isolation and marginalisation for black and Asian offenders in mixed probation groups. Denney (1992), for example, reports the results of a study of a group-work programme which found that black men and women often found it difficult to relate to others in the groups and that some black and Asian clients reported feelings of isolation and disconnection in their mixed probation groups. However, no information is given as to the sample size of study participants and so it is impossible to evaluate the significance of the views expressed.

More recent research on mixed group-work programmes in the prison service involved interviews with black prisoners drawn from 14 different prisons. This found that a significant number of black prisoners felt that they would have had a more positive experience if they had not been the sole black member of the group (Akhtar, 2001). Earlier research by Fisher and Watkins (1993) recorded the experiences of a mixed offending behaviour group in Wandsworth Prison. They also suggested that there should at least be more than one black member in a mixed group to reduce the possible sense of isolation that one black person on his own might experience. They were concerned that, if black members in the group were a minority, they may feel less able to discuss issues from their perspective. However, this was only speculation by the authors and was not based on any empirical evidence. A document published by the Inner London Probation Service based on many workshops with ILPS' practice teachers also notes that encouraging a black student to participate in a discussion on race with a predominantly white group of students exposes them to the potential for further racism (ILPS, 1993). It may be possible to draw parallels between the experience of women in groups made up mainly of men and minority ethnic offenders in mixed race groups. There is evidence that, where women are a minority, their needs are submerged (Mistry, 1993).

On the other hand, research has found that groups with a significant number of black and Asian members, or that are all black and Asian, can be more supportive. Offenders can give support to each other and can develop 'a sense of belonging' especially when the positive experiences of some minority ethnic members (e.g. in jobs) gives encouragement to others who doubt their chances of succeeding within a hostile system (Raynor et al., 1994; Fisher and Watkins, 1993). Again, drawing a parallel with gender, it has also been found that women in all female groups are able to develop a support system and give each other emotional and practical help (Mistry, 1993).

Arguments against separate provision

It should not be assumed that all minority ethnic offenders want to be in separate provision. A recent study based on interviews with black offenders found that they did not like the idea of all black groups. They felt that it was unfair segregation and that they were being picked out, saying for example 'No, that's segregation...' or 'That's just picking us out'. They also felt that they had had the same experiences as white offenders and so there was no need for separate groups (Tuklo Orenda Associates, 1999). However, the study does not say how many black offenders were interviewed and so it is difficult to evaluate the significance of the responses. Other recent research on mixed group-work programmes in the prison service also found from interviews with black prisoners drawn from 14 prisons that, despite not wanting to be the sole ethnic minority member, most would still have mixed groups which include both black and white members (Akhtar, 2001). However, care needs to be taken in interpreting these findings because offenders may reply inaccurately to avoid drawing attention to themselves as being different if white researchers conduct interviews. Reponses may also differ depending on the way questions are asked.

There is some evidence that mixed groups can work well. The INSIGHT young offenders project in south-east London stressed the fundamental similarity of black people and other groups of people and aimed to prepare students to undertake a further or higher education programme upon completion of the course. It had very good results with mixed groups; however, positive outcomes for black people are affected by their tutors' personal beliefs, preparedness, integrity, commitment to non-oppressive casework strategies, resource availability and high motivation levels (Lawrence, 1995).

Two further points need to be considered. Firstly, where separate provision exists, the Probation Service must guard against the risk that black offenders may be automatically referred to a specialist black and Asian project if one exists, regardless of their individual circumstances (NACRO, 1991). Secondly, white offenders may feel an injustice if black offenders are given particular types of training or rehabilitation, especially if the white people suffer similar inequalities (Dominelli et al., 1995).

Other considerations

1) The distribution of ethnic minority communities in the UK

Minority ethnic communities in the UK are clustered within areas. For example, nearly half (46%) of ethnic minority offenders starting probation in 1998/99 were supervised by just five Probation Services (Inner London, Middlesex, North East London, South East London and South West London). Inner London Probation Service alone supervised one-quarter of ethnic minority offenders on probation. In contrast, other services supervised very small numbers of offenders. 1998 Probation Statistics show that less than one per cent of offenders starting probation supervision were from minority ethnic groups in Cumbria, Devon, Cornwall, Kent, Lincolnshire, Shropshire, Teesside, North Yorkshire, Dyfed, North Wales, Mid Glamorgan and West Glamorgan. Areas supervising small numbers of black and Asian offenders are unlikely in practice to be able to offer separate group provision. Therefore other opportunities will need to be made available such as one-to-one programmes delivered by specially trained staff and/or offering support such as mentors to those doing accredited offending behaviour programmes in mixed groups.

2) Mixed race offenders

Groups specifically for black and Asian offenders or white offenders can be difficult for offenders of mixed race who may feel isolated in either black or white groups (Tuklo Orenda Associates, 1999). For example, during interviews about a black empowerment group run by Inner London Probation Service, some of those who saw themselves as being of mixed race felt that the sessions were too 'black'. They said that they still felt like a minority within these groups and did not fit in (ILPS, 1996).

Conclusions

The Probation Service deals with more black and fewer Asian offenders than would be expected from their distribution in the general population. There is no evidence that black and Asian offenders have unique criminogenic needs. It is, however, possible that combined effects of the relative deprivation of their communities and institutional racism mean that they are both less able to achieve their goals through legitimate means and are more likely to experience one or more factors that puts them at risk of offending. Further research is currently being done to establish the criminogenic needs of black and Asian offenders on probation. This will also establish if these needs are different or if they are experienced to a greater or lesser extent than among white offenders.

It is difficult to draw any firm conclusions from previous research about the appropriateness of separate provision for black and Asian offenders on probation. There are many arguments that support running separate programmes but also some that advocate mixed group-work provision. There is, as yet, little empirical evidence to substantiate either position. Ongoing research to evaluate the effectiveness of a variety of offending programmes by the Universities of Leicester and Liverpool will establish if outcomes for black and Asian offenders are different to those for white offenders in the same groups. However, it is clear that groups including only one or two black and Asian offenders are unlikely to be effective in addressing those offenders' needs due to feelings of isolation and disconnection.

3. The extent and nature of existing group-work provision for black and Asian offenders

Previous research has found very few group-work programmes specifically for black and Asian offenders. For example, in a survey of 1463 groups, only three were black or Asian membership-only (Caddick, 1993)[12]. It has been suggested that, not only are black or Asian-only groups a 'rare phenomenon', but there is no evidence that any groups give central concern to the differential needs of black, Asian and white offenders (Senior, 1993:39).

Two probation programmes for black and Asian offenders have been documented in the published literature. The Black Offenders Initiative set up by the North Thames Resource Unit developed a programme aimed at empowerment and the exploration of black and Asian offenders' experiences. Although it had not been robustly evaluated at the time of writing, it had received positive feedback from both the members and the leaders of the three groups who had completed it (Raynor *et al.*, 1994). Another programme, run recently in Moss Side by Greater Manchester Probation Service, targeted offenders involved in drug supply and addressed issues such as policing and rights, pressures, racism, alternatives to offending and opportunities. Although not set up specifically for black offenders, members were predominantly from the local black community. The project involved people from community groups and was said to create a positive atmosphere within the local community. Feedback from offenders and programme facilitators was also positive. Project participants are reported to have subsequently attended college, work or have re-established themselves in business (Briggs, 1995; Briggs, 1996; Brown and Poole, 1997).

Tuklo Orenda Associates (1999) prepared a handbook for South West Probation Training Consortium entitled *Making a Difference: A Positive and Practical Guide to Working with Black Offenders*. Drawing on information from practitioners in the south-west area, it gives extensive guidance on the best way to work with black offenders. Strategies identified range from the need to understand racism to the acknowledgement of the differences between black and white values, learning styles, language and manner.

---

12. The survey was conducted over ten years ago and included more than three-quarters of all the Probation Services in England and Wales.

The current position

Faced with this lack of information, a survey was conducted to identify the extent of current probation work specifically with black and Asian offenders. The survey was sent to all Probation Services in England and Wales in June 2000. Forty-five of the 54 (83%) Probation Services responded.

The survey identified 13 programmes in ten services that had been developed specifically to target black and Asian offenders. Five were running at the time the survey was conducted. A further nine of the 45 services reported that they planned to introduce a programme for black and Asian offenders. These services were Berkshire, Greater Manchester, Inner London, Leicestershire and Rutland, Merseyside, North East London, South East London, South Glamorgan and West Midlands. Gloucestershire Probation Service was not sure if it would run a programme in the future.

Nearly half the services (46%) reported having established links with partnership organisations to work specifically with this offender group. Services were also asked whether interventions with black and Asian offenders were noted as a priority in their local Crime and Disorder Strategies; a third (33%) of services reported this to be a priority. However, this is not backed up by other research on crime and disorder strategies (see Phillips *et al.*, 2000).

Case studies

In order to find out about the content of programmes that were being delivered to black and Asian offenders and to explore the views of people who had worked on the programmes, we visited ten of the 13 programmes[13] identified by the survey were visited. In total 28 members of staff[14] who had been, or were currently involved in designing, delivering and managing the programmes were interviewed. The interviews included both descriptions of the intervention and also staff views on the factors that contributed to its success or failure.

---

13.   Three further programmes were identified in Merseyside, South Glamorgan and North East London Probation Services. Merseyside Probation Service had developed a black empowerment programme but this was not delivered to any offenders. Interviews there focused on the contents of the course and establishing why it had not been delivered. The South Glamorgan black offender programme was still under development at the time of interviews. It was not possible to interview developers and facilitators of the North East London Probation Service black empowerment group as key members of staff were on long-term leave.

14.   Those interviewed included 15 Probation Officers, seven Senior Probation Officers, three Researchers, two Assistant Chief Probation Officers and one Consultant/Trainer.

Very few views of senior management were sought and there were no interviews with offenders who had attended the programmes[15]. This is an important limitation to this study as it would be useful to be able to marry the views of probation staff with those of offenders and of probation service managers. Where possible, Chapter 4 reports any information that had been collected and written up about outcomes for offenders on the programmes or any other measure of effectiveness.

Four types of approaches to delivering group-work programmes to black and Asian offenders were identified:

- *Black empowerment groups* (three of ten)
  These were stand-alone programmes specifically designed to address issues of racism and how this relates to offending behaviour;
- *Black empowerment within general offending programmes* (four of ten)
  Here black empowerment groups formed a module within a longer general offending programme. Participation was generally seen either as preparation for the offending behaviour programme or as reinforcement;
- *Black empowerment and reintegration programmes* (one of ten)
  This was a black empowerment programme with additional work targeting education, training and employment needs; and
- *Offence specific programmes* (two of ten)
  Both targeted Asian males who had been convicted of drink-drive offences

Table 3.1 summarises the content of the programmes for black and Asian offenders. Appendix 1 has detailed descriptions of each programme.

Characteristics of participants

Seven out of ten programmes were exclusively for men. While the others were open to female participants, in practice they mainly received referrals for men. All the women who had been accepted to the programmes attended groups where the majority of participants were men. Surprisingly, programme deliverers stressed that women who had attended courses had not experienced any problems in being in the minority[16]. This is contrary to

---

15. The Home Office has commissioned another research project to explore the views and experiences of black and Asian offenders on probation. This study includes offenders who have done programmes as well as more general probation supervision.
16. It is important to note that this was the interviewees' perception of the women's views and it is possible that the women themselves may have felt differently.

Table 3.1: Summary of the case studies

Programme name and area delivered	Still running	Type of programme (self-defined by services)	Theory basis	Offender group	Target offence by risk[1]	No. of sessions	Use mentors or outside speakers	Formal evaluation conducted
Black Offending Behaviour Programme *Greater Manchester Probation Service*	Yes	Empowerment and general offending	● Cognitive-behavioural ● Educational ● Empowerment	Male Minority ethnic	Yes	26	Yes	Yes
Black Self Development and Educational Attainment Group *Inner London Probation Service*	Yes	Empowerment and reintegration	● Cognitive behavioural ● Educational ● Empowerment ● Control	Mixed gender Minority ethnic	Yes	20	Yes	Yes
Black Self Development Programme *Inner London Probation Service*	Yes	Empowerment and general offending	● Cognitive behavioural ● Educational ● Empowerment ● Pro-social	Male Minority ethnic	Yes	12	No	No
Black Probation Group *South East London Probation Service*	Yes	Empowerment	● Cognitive behavioural ● Empowerment	Mixed gender Minority ethnic	No	10	No	No
Black People and Offending *West Midlands Probation Service*	Yes	Empowerment	● Cognitive behavioural ● Pro-social ● Empowerment	Male Minority ethnic	No	12	No	Yes

Programme name and area delivered	Still running	Type of programme (self-defined by services)	Theory basis	Offender group	Target offence by risk[1]	No. of sessions	Use mentors or outside speakers	Formal evaluation conducted
Asian Alcohol Impaired Drivers *Leicestershire and Rutland*	No	Offence focused	• Cognitive behavioural • Educational	Male Asian	Yes	6	Yes	Yes
Group for Asian Drink-Drivers *West Midlands Probation Service*	No	Offence focused	• Cognitive behavioural • Pro-social • Educational	Male Asian	No	6	No	No
Black Offender Programme *West Yorkshire Probation Service*	No	Empowerment and general offending	• Cognitive behavioural • Educational • Empowerment • Control	Male Minority ethnic	Yes	16	Yes	No
Face the Future Programme *West Yorkshire*	No	Empowerment and general offending	• Cognitive behavioural • Educational • Empowerment	Male Minority ethnic	Yes	35	Yes	No
Black Empowerment Group *Hereford and Worcester*	No	Empowerment	• Cognitive behavioural • Educational	Mixed gender Minority ethnic	No	4	No	No

Note
1. This refers to whether the programme targeted offenders who had a specific level of risk of reoffending, e.g. low, medium or high-risk offenders.

most of the research that emphasises the difficulties women may experience when in the minority (Mistry, 1993). Staff said that women were assessed prior to attending the group to ensure they would benefit from the programme and not feel marginalised. Staff who worked with groups with a gender mix of offenders reported that the skill of the facilitator was important to ensure the needs of the women were being met.

Groups included offenders with a wide age range, although most participants were aged between 20 and 30. Most facilitators felt that having such a broad age range of programme attendees was beneficial, as older offenders could demonstrate to younger offenders the negative consequences of a life of crime:

> If there are older people in the groups it does tend to work quite well. The older ones will say to the younger ones 'look do you really want to keep coming back? Don't make the same mistakes I have'.

Six programmes targeted offenders according to their risk of reoffending: generally medium to high-risk offenders who were also at risk of receiving a custodial sentence. Programmes that were still in existence were more likely to target offenders in this way: four out of five programmes currently running targeted according to risk, compared to only two of five programmes no longer in existence. This difference between current programmes and those set up some time ago is unsurprising given that the 'What Works' strategy currently emphasises the importance of targeting interventions according to an assessment of the offender's risk of reoffending or of causing harm.

Theoretical basis

Most of the programmes for black and Asian offenders drew on a combination of different theories including cognitive-behavioural, educational, control theory, and empowerment[17]. Interviewees generally thought that programmes for black and Asian offenders required an eclectic approach encompassing a range of different theories:

> ...it's not just cognitive-behavioural, it's far more holistic. You have to look at the whole social context...you really need a holistic approach because you are dealing with far more complex issues.

---

17.   These theories are explained in Appendix 2.

Many of those involved in the development of interventions said that they found it difficult to find a suitable theory for working with this group of offenders. They recognised that the lack of published research about 'What Works' with black and Asian offenders meant that there is no single theory that has a strong evidence-base of its effectiveness with this client group. Programme developers often resorted to drawing on their own experience of working with offenders to identify theories that were likely to be effective. Half the programmes (five out of ten) employed an external consultant to help develop the programme. Unsurprisingly, those that used consultants tended to have a more sophisticated theoretical basis. It must be remembered that some of the staff interviewed started developing these programmes up to ten years earlier and that the nature of programme development and delivery has changed considerably within the Probation Service since then. In many cases, programmes were set up prior to the introduction of the 'What Works' strategy which has now become an integral part of the working of the Probation Service and requires group-work programmes to be both evidenced-based and have a strong theoretical background. Programmes that were still being delivered had, in most cases, been further developed and refined in light of the 'What Works' strategy so that they have a theoretical basis and draw upon the little existing research into effective practice with black and Asian offenders. They tended to be based on cognitive-behavioural theories that have been identified as being successful with a wide range of different offenders (Vennard and Hedderman, 1998)[18].

Staff delivering both the offence-specific programmes reported having adapted an existing programme to make it culturally relevant. They felt that this had been an effective way of delivering such a programme to black and Asian offenders.

Ethnicity of programme participants

Most groups were open to both black and Asian offenders and participants tended to come from a range of different ethnic backgrounds. Some groups were less specific about ethnic background and were open to anyone who had a 'common experience of racism and discrimination'.

Facilitators felt that, as the groups were comprised of minority ethnic offenders and facilitators who had all been the victims of racism, it provided a safe, supportive environment for offenders to discuss sensitive issues around racism, particularly how this had

---

18. The Home Office has commissioned a number of studies to evaluate the effectiveness of various offending behaviour programmes based on cognitive-behavioural theories. One of the important findings that will come from these studies is an understanding of whether these are equally effective for offenders from minority groups.

impacted on their lives and offending behaviour. It was felt that groups including white offenders were often characterised by undercurrents of racism that made it difficult for black and Asian offenders to address issues of racism and the impact this may have on their offending behaviour:

> ...where you have mixed groups, it's often quite unsafe for black offenders being in there, especially if they're the only one, or just one or two of them and 20 others. Some may be quite racist and hostile and may not give them the space. In that sort of an environment, the last thing you're going to think about is your offending, you're just going to be thinking about surviving.

There were also difficulties in groups made up of offenders from a diversity of minority ethnic groups. These were recognised as being more challenging to the facilitator who had to ensure the needs of all attendees were being met and that their culture was being represented in the course:

> If you have a group, for example, where there is one Asian person in a group of African/Caribbeans, you have to work much harder to ensure that person is included. You also have to make sure you really do some research to understand the different cultures that are represented in the group.

On the basis of their experience of running programmes, staff said that having both black and Asian offenders in the same group could sometimes be problematic. They saw the main problems as that racism sometimes existed between the two cultures and Asian offenders, who were often in the minority, might feel marginalised:

> I think that it was the fact that it was an all Asian environment that made the men stick with it .... It was Asians running a programme for Asians.

On the other hand, some programme deliverers felt that culturally diverse groups were more effective. They suggested that the group participants all had common experiences of racism that they could share, the group would challenge their own prejudicial views and it provided an opportunity for offenders to learn about other cultures.

Only two programmes were identified that were exclusively for Asian offenders and neither were delivering courses to offenders at the time of interview. Staff who had facilitated courses that only targeted Asian offenders felt strongly that there was a need for separate, specialist provision for this group for several reasons. Firstly, Asian offenders were often in the minority in predominantly black offender groups which can lead to them feeling marginalised and their needs not being adequately met. They also felt that Asian offenders had different criminogenic needs and committed different offences to black offenders. Finally, staff considered specialist provision necessary for Asian offenders because they had different cultural, religious and historical backgrounds, all of which were integral topics in such programmes. They felt that the only common factor among black and Asian offenders was the experience of racism:

> If you look at the types of crimes that black offenders are committing and the types of crimes that Asian males are committing, they are very different. The causes of Asian people offending are very different to the causes of black people offending. You can't address all their needs in a single group. They have some common experiences, for example, they have both experienced discrimination, but that's where it stops.

Staff who had developed programmes that were delivered to both black and Asian offenders tried to address some of the problems associated with mixed groups in their programme design. Many had been designed to be culturally relevant to a diversity of ethnic groups and allowed facilitators to adapt the course contents according to the group participants. Several facilitators and managers said that they would prefer to have separate provision for members of different ethnic minority groups but reported that the small numbers of Asian offenders in their service meant that it would be impossible to deliver separate group-work. One programme was trying to reduce the problems associated with providing for Asian offenders in multi-ethnic groups by seeking to recruit Asian staff to the programme, either as facilitators or as mentors.

Clearly, the issue of placing offenders from different minority ethnic backgrounds within the same group is complex. There was no overall consensus among staff as to whether it was better to provide separate programmes for each ethnic group or to provide a single programme for all offenders identified as being from a minority ethnic background. However, most staff agreed that the facilitator's skills were vital to ensure that all offenders' needs were met in a mixed group.

Delivery of programmes

Dosage

Programmes varied in their intensity and length. Some programmes were short and consisted of four sessions, delivered once weekly. Others were over 20 sessions in length and delivered several times a week. Staff involved in delivering shorter programmes reported often having insufficient time to cover all the issues that the programme raised. This was particularly noted on programmes only delivering a black empowerment module and those that were offence-specific.

Facilitators generally felt that longer, more intensive programmes were more successful as they allowed time for group members to become more involved in the programme and have a greater commitment to attend, participate and provide mutual support. Interviewees indicated that the best results were achieved with these programmes and that retention of offenders on longer programmes actually increased. Generally, probation supervision is increasingly incorporating a number of interventions based on an assessment of need. Not all black and Asian offenders will be assessed as having a need for this type of programme. However, the benefits of longer programmes have to be set against the potential risk that, the design of some interventions (e.g. where black and Asian offenders do additional modules to a general offending behaviour programme) may raise questions of unequal treatment as they will be subject to more intensive requirements in their order than comparable white offenders and be subjected to a greater loss of liberty. To avoid this risk, it will be important that there is a thorough assessment of need.

Teaching style

An active participation teaching style was adopted by all the programmes and has been found elsewhere to be effective with most types of offenders (Andrews, 1995). Facilitators reported that this was the most effective way of working with this offender group, as it increased their engagement in the programme and their ability to learn. They believed that this was particularly important with black and Asian offenders because of their poor educational experiences.

The style of teaching we use is to make the offenders involved. We realised from the first session that the way to engage black offenders was to involve them, rather than them just sitting and listening, make the sessions participatory.

Targeting

Most of the staff interviewed noted the importance of effective targeting. Staff generally agreed that programmes that targeted offenders likely to benefit from the programme and who could demonstrate a motivation to change had a greater proportion of successful completions. They did not think that the programmes would benefit all black and Asian offenders. Other factors such as the type of offence and whether their offending behaviour is related to their experience of being black or Asian were considered to be important:

It depends on what they have done and what their key issues are. I don't believe that if someone has been drive-disqualified or their key problem is temper control, that you should then say because they are black or Asian they should go into this group. If temper control is the issue, then temper control is the group they should attend.

Programme integrity

Most interviewees also considered programme integrity to be important to the success of programmes. In some cases integrity was being formally monitored either by staff completing integrity checklists or, in a minority of cases, video recording sessions. Programmes that were still running tended to be more likely to have systems in place to monitor integrity, probably influenced by the wider 'What Works' strategy which emphasises the importance of programme integrity in offending programmes more generally.

Management support

Those areas that had had good management support for their programme were more likely to still be delivering the programme. It has been generally recognised that offending behaviour programmes with full management support are likely to be more effective (Vennard and Hedderman, 1998). Programmes that were still running at the time of interview were those where the service as a whole was committed to the intervention and were not reliant on one or two dedicated staff members.

Many staff interviewed expressed dissatisfaction with the level of support they had received from service management when developing and delivering the programmes, but it was not possible to discuss their views with many senior managers because of the limited scope of this study. The quotes below illustrate staff views of management support:

Management support had been very poor. Their attitude is that we are giving you something, but they don't realise they aren't giving us something, they are giving the service something that is going to benefit the clients. The management has to make the commitment to see things through in a fashion that will allow it to sustain itself. If certain things are not put into place, it will not be sustainable.

Absolutely not enough [management support]. They don't understand the programme; they ask the most stupid questions. Their pro-social modelling is not good; they are not putting into place effective practice. They can treat black staff

23

quite appallingly. They don't consult properly, they don't ask the right questions, they just go ahead and do what they feel is appropriate.

Most interviewees also felt that resource provision had been inadequate to ensure good development, delivery, monitoring and evaluation. Staff felt particularly dissatisfied with the level of resources in services where management had recognised the need and sanctioned the delivery of a group-work programme to black and Asian offenders. Often they said that resource provision was less than that allocated to other offending behaviour programmes delivered by the service. Some facilitators said that services such as translators and interpreters were not available. These were important in order to create course materials that reflect the composition of the group and the cultural diversity in this country (Akhtar, 2001; Lawrence, 1995; Denney, 1992). Without access to interpreters, groups are less available to black and Asian offenders who have difficulties with the English language (Denney, 1992; NAPO, 1988; Central Council of Probation Committees Steering Group on Inner Cities, 1983; Taylor, 1981).

Several interviewees reported that programme development had been constrained by a lack of resources, e.g. making it impossible for them to ask for advice from an academic consultant or recruit appropriate staff to deliver the programme. Again these staff felt that resource provision was less than that allocated to other programmes. The fact that this study did not explore the views of many senior managers or collect information about costs, means that it is not possible to comment on whether this feeling is justified. In some cases, changes in resource allocation had led to programmes being terminated, as they were not considered to be cost-effective.

Interviewees were critical of the extent of negotiation and consultation they had to engage in with service management for the programme to be established as an integral part of service group-work provision. In many cases, staff felt that they had had to have greater negotiation with service management because the programme idea had originated from members of staff who had recognised a need for such a programme, rather than a service initiative:

A lot of the initiatives for black offenders have come from the staff; it hasn't been a service commitment to provide something for black offenders. This makes it harder to get what you want. Services should be leading on this, not staff. At the moment it's a bottom up approach.

Lack of management commitment to the programme was sometimes cited as a reason for its collapse, either because management decided to stop the programme and move resources elsewhere or because staff who had set up the intervention refused to continue running the programme because of lack of support. Again, however, Probation Services managers' views on this were not explored.

Many staff criticised the amount of time they had been given to develop programmes. Most said that they had been given little or no relief from their existing workload and often conducted most of the development work in their own time:

> There have also been more problems with management support in terms of developing the manual. It's taken a lot of work to do and management haven't given us enough time or space, they always want to rush things through. They want us to work on it in our own time. We haven't been given any relief from work to do it. In a way, that is very much how black self-development has grown and failed in the past.

Even staff who had the full support of their managers and where the establishment of a programme for black and Asian offenders was an area initiative, criticised the amount of time allocated to development. Programme deliverers reported that they were given little or no time to prepare for each session and practise exercises. Several facilitators reported reading exercises for the first time while actually delivering sessions.

Staff training and supervision

Training to develop and deliver programmes was generally considered to be inadequate. Many staff said that they had little or, in many cases, no training in working with black and Asian offenders. This was often despite staff specifically requesting training in this area.

This appears to conflict with replies from the survey which indicated that most services provide staff training in issues relating to racism: 93 per cent offered training in equal opportunities and 84 per cent in racism awareness. However, services were not asked to describe the content of the training or the numbers of staff undertaking the training. The HMIP (2000) Thematic Inspection Report on race found that, although staff at all levels in every service emphasised the importance of training on race in relation to service delivery, little such training was available. Only 22 services provided training on work with minority ethnic offenders. It is likely that people involved in programme delivery have different training needs from those of probation officers working with black and Asian offenders individually. Previous research has argued that training in cultural studies and anti-racism should be improved for staff working with black and Asian offenders. This should be provided for all probation staff, not just those responsible for delivering programmes (Akhtar, 2001; Frances-Spence, 1995; Kett *et al.*, 1991; NACRO, 1991; Day *et al.*, 1989; NAPO, 1988; Taylor, 1981). Specialised training will be required for those delivering programmes for black and Asian offenders.

Supervision of tutors was also considered to be inadequate leading, on one occasion, to staff feeling unable to continue delivering the programme and resulting in its collapse. Guidance was issued to Chief Probation Officers in 1995 that stressed the importance of staff training, supervision and adequate resource provision but HMIP (2000) found that black and Asian staff feel particularly unsupported.

Programme staff reported insufficient recruitment of appropriate staff to facilitate the groups. They often believed that this was because posts were not actively advertised and because inadequate training was provided for staff to deliver programmes effectively.

It was particularly difficult to recruit staff to deliver programmes for Asian offenders because Asian staff are under-represented within the Probation Service[19]. One of the programmes identified that targeted Asian offenders was no longer running as a key member of staff had left and had not been replaced. One respondent noted that services located in areas where the population is made up of a high number of Asian people need to be particularly pro-active in recruiting more Asian staff. Other writers[20] have reported that recruiting greater numbers of black and Asian probation staff should be a service priority, although the numbers of Probation Service staff from minority ethnic groups has increased in recent years (Probation Statistics 1999, Figure 8). Further research is required into the retention and promotion of black and Asian staff within the Probation Service, particularly as they are under-represented at chief officer level and other management grades (HMIP, 2000).

The role of the facilitator

The skill, commitment and dedication of the programme deliverers was vital to the setting up and survival of programmes. For example, referring sufficient numbers of offenders to programmes was often because dedicated course tutors would actively seek out new referrals and promote the programme. The enthusiasm of tutors was also reflected in the

19.   Minority ethnic groups made up 9.3 per cent of all probation staff at the end of 1999. There were proportionately three times as many black staff as in the general population and half as many South Asians (Probation Statistics 1999 p. 11).

20.   ILPS, 1996; Dominelli *et al.*, 1995; Frances-Spence, 1995; Raynor *et al.*, 1994; Denney, 1992; NACRO, 1991; Day *et al.*, 1989; Central Council of Probation Committees Steering Group on Inner Cities, 1983; Taylor, 1981.

commitment of offenders to attend the programme: most staff thought that the low drop-out rates experienced by many programmes were largely due to the ability of the facilitators to engage men in the course. Replicating pilot programmes' success as they become part of mainstream work is a problem that faces all developmental projects. Partly, this is because the pioneers who start new initiatives are often especially enthusiastic and committed to the programmes. Measures to enable success to continue include developing manuals and course materials, training and recognising the competencies required in facilitators.

Ethnicity of the facilitator

It was generally agreed that programme deliverers should be of a similar minority ethnic background as the group participants. However, it is difficult to achieve this kind of 'match' between the facilitator(s) and participants where the group comprises of offenders from many different ethnic backgrounds. Virtually all staff interviewed felt that programme staff should be from a minority ethnic background so that facilitators would provide positive role models to offenders. They also had common experiences of racism that they could share with group participants and were considered to have a greater empathy and understanding of these clients. Interviewees also thought that, because tutors had a greater knowledge of minority ethnic cultures, they would be more likely to identify situations when an offender would reoffend. This was considered especially important when working with Asian drink-driving offenders. Two of the 13 programmes identified were not run exclusively by black officers. Both of these folded because of low take-up rates. A study by Inner London Probation Service (1996) reported that black offenders felt it was important to have black staff available to talk to, as they were better able to relate to the offender.

However, many of those interviewed stressed that being of the same ethnic background as programme participants was not sufficient criterion to be a tutor on courses for black and Asian offenders. They felt it was important for facilitators to have a good understanding of racism and its impact on an offender's behaviour. Tutors needed also to have considered the impact of racism on their own behaviour and to have resolved any issues they may have around such experiences. They also need a good understanding of their own culture and other minority ethnic cultures:

> Staff have to undertake a lot of learning in what black self-development means, both personally and professionally. As a practitioner within a group you need to be confident and have sorted out your own ideas enough to deal with challenges from the rest of the group.

Some services had difficulty recruiting staff to deliver programmes combining a general offending programme with a black empowerment component. Interviewees thought that this was because potential applicants did not think that the programmes concentrated sufficiently on culture and race. Staff running such programmes thought that focusing too much on culture would be unmanageable, especially where there were considerable ethnic diversities in the groups. They wanted to keep the focus of the programme on offending behaviour.

Generally, interviewees believed it was important to have both male and female facilitators delivering the programmes to reduce any sense of collusion between facilitators and offenders in all male groups. This was also important for programmes which women could attend but were often in the minority.

Using invited speakers and mentors

Many writers have urged greater liaison between Probation Services and black community members. Probation Services should draw on the expertise of organisations and individuals within black communities (Tuklo Orenda Associates, 1999; Denney, 1992; Kett et al., 1991; NACRO, 1991; Day et al., 1989; NAPO, 1988). Most programmes invited speakers from the community to come and speak to the offenders. They were usually of a minority ethnic background and were either successful professionals such as lawyers or doctors, business men and women or people working in services that may be of use to offenders (e.g. employment services and drug services). Professionals were invited to the programmes to provide positive role models and talk to the group about their own experiences of racism and how they had coped with them. Service providers were invited to the group to show offenders the range of community support services that are available to them and encourage them to utilise such services. It was generally agreed that using invited speakers was a positive aspect of the programmes and benefited offenders greatly.

Two programmes had also implemented mentoring schemes in which mentors of the same ethnic background as the offender attended the groups with the offender. They would provide additional support to the participant, where issues raised in the group had not been resolved. Mentors would be assigned to the offender throughout the entire probation order and would help the offender gain access to other services and support them when seeking work and training. Mentoring schemes were considered to be an important factor in the success of programmes. However, ensuring that mentors were appropriately placed with offenders required a considerable amount of organisation. It was important that a staff member was assigned this responsibility and given adequate time to co-ordinate the scheme. Several of the groups still running that did not provide mentoring were considering implementing such schemes. Mentors are also supporting black and Asian offenders who are doing general offending programmes in mixed groups (e.g. Merseyside).

Referrals

Low referral rates had threatened the survival of most programmes and were a contributory factor to the failure of many of the programmes that were no longer running. The ability to reach sufficient numbers of offenders to run the programme often depended on the dedication of course tutors actively to seek out potential participants and advertise the programme to PSR writers and sentencers. Interviewees were concerned about the low levels of referrals as they noted the disproportionately high number of black offenders in the criminal justice system.

One of the reasons offered for low referrals was a lack of management commitment to ensure adequate referrals were made to the programme. It was felt that if management were more committed to the programme and had developed systems to ensure all appropriate offenders were being referred, rates would be considerably higher:

> I think we would've got more referrals had management been more pro-active and more involved. There was no structure for referrals. Management should've overseen the process of referrals but they didn't.

Insufficient publicity of programmes was also considered to be a factor in low referral rates. Several course tutors felt that their programmes had not been sufficiently well promoted to those who would be making referrals to the course.

Many interviewees also reported that probation staff and courts were reluctant to refer offenders to the programmes. They believed that this was because many probation officers and sentencers did not believe that separate or specialist provision was necessary:

> There were political problems around the group, specifically around people questioning why we should have a group for black-only offenders. ...Two [magistrates] said they weren't even prepared to consider it. So there was a lot of blatant 'we're not supporting this'.

Some staff thought the low referral rates by fellow workers and the courts were because they did not understand the groups' purpose or what happened in the sessions. This led to other probation officers, particularly officers who were not of the same ethnic background as course facilitators, feeling threatened by the group. It has been reported elsewhere that if programmes are to receive adequate referrals, services need to publicise their programme's contents, aims and objectives to all potential referrers (Taylor, 1981).

Lack of training for white probation officers in their work with black and Asian offenders was considered to be a factor in the low referral rates. Interviewees thought that white officers were reluctant to address issues relating to racism and ethnicity and suggest separate or specialist provision to offenders for fear of appearing racist:

> [Low referrals] *can be a problem because white probation officers have only had minimal training and what they have had has raised their anxieties. They can often be worried about bringing the subject up of the offender being black in case they are perceived as being racist.*

A few of those interviewed noted that greater numbers of black and Asian offenders in their services were being sentenced to community service orders rather than probation orders. These staff suggested that fewer black and Asian offenders were being placed on probation orders because PSR writers mainly recommended white offenders for probation orders as they felt they would be easier to supervise than black and Asian offenders:

> *There was a problem in getting probation officers to refer black offenders to the programme. I think it actually comes down to the probation officer saying 'can I work with this person, or do I want them to go off and work somewhere else?' They tended to send them to do community service rather than send them on individual programmes, because if you looked at numbers of black and Asians doing community service, it was really high.*

This could be considered a form of institutional racism. Previous research has found that fewer recommendations for community supervision were made by probation officers on black offenders, resulting in a disproportionate number being imprisoned (Green, 1989).

Monitoring and evaluation

Programmes varied in the quality of monitoring and evaluation arrangements they had in place, but generally this was poor. Many had little or no evaluation work completed on them. Staff often felt that this was due to lack of resources. They felt they had not been allocated sufficient time or been given training to evaluate the programmes. While many programme deliverers collected feedback sheets after each session from offenders, often they did not collate or analyse the responses.

The four programmes which had been evaluated all ran in large services areas that had internal research departments. They also tended to be the programmes that had greater management support and commitment to running the intervention. Unfortunately, the evaluations that had been conducted were based on small sample sizes, and therefore the findings should be treated with caution. Only two of the programmes identified had conducted a reconviction analysis of offenders completing the course. None of the services had yet evaluated the cost-effectiveness of their programme. (The evidence about the effectiveness of the programmes is discussed in Chapter 4.)

Case management

Arrangements for case management varied between the programmes identified. Some programme deliverers were critical that issues brought up during the intervention were not followed through in the rest of the order. This is especially important if issues were not completely resolved during the programme, perhaps due to time constraints, and required further input. A minority of programmes had begun exploring ways of overcoming this e.g. setting up call-back sessions. Another area had set up a feedback system in which the group leader and the offender jointly compiled a report of achievements during the programme and a list of things they would still like to achieve. This could be fed back to their supervising officer. The service employing this feedback system was positive about its benefits as they felt it assisted the offender in identifying and communicating needs still to be met and helped the case manger understand the programme's contents:

The clients feel more empowered at the end of the programme to say, 'this is what I want'. Clients were often reporting having communication problems with their officers in explaining what they wanted, so the report was seen as an aid to this. It also helps officers to understand what's been going on in the group.

It is important to recognise that the problem of how best to encompass the work done in programmes into the whole period of an offender's supervision is not restricted to programmes for black and Asian offenders. For example, the Think First general offending programme includes a three-way meeting between the group leader, offender and case manager which takes place at the end of the programme. However, an early evaluation in Thames Valley has found that case managers often did not attend these meetings. The area is doing further work to encourage attendance and generally build on the offender's experience of Think First in the remainder of their supervision (National Probation Service Thames Valley Research and Evaluation Unit, 2001).

4.   The effectiveness of programmes for black and Asian offenders

As few programmes had been subject to monitoring and evaluation, it is difficult to make any conclusions about their effectiveness based on outcomes for offenders or to decide if separate, specialist programmes are more effective in reducing offending by black and Asian offenders than mixed, general provision. This Chapter reports the views of the programme developers and deliverers and reviews the three evaluations that have taken place to date.

Staffs' views on programme effectiveness

All the staff interviewed were committed to running such programmes and strongly believed that they were effective in reducing reoffending. They felt that the offenders' enjoyment of the programme was evident by the low drop-out rates and the positive feedback received from participants.

> *Attendance is always very good to the programme. I have not had to breach[21] a single black client who has been on the programme.*

> *Feedback from offenders was very positive. Many of them were really fired up and enthusiastic at the end about looking for a job. Their commitment to attending was good.*

Many staff said that they had noted changes in offenders' attitudes and behaviour during the course of the intervention and received anecdotal evidence that participants went on to find employment or training. Staff suggested that minority ethnic offenders who attended the programmes appeared to have better experiences and outcomes as a result of the programmes than white offenders who attended similar offending behaviour groups. The quotes below highlight some of the benefits that offenders were perceived to gain from the programmes:

---

21.   Breach action, where the offender is returned to court, may be taken on any offender who fails to comply with a community sentence and is not able to give an acceptable explanation. Breach procedures have changed in recent years. Currently, breach procedures may start after one unacceptable failure, where appropriate, but **must** be commenced no later than the third failure to comply with the requirement of an order.

Clearly offenders are getting something out of it because even with the intensity of the programme, offenders have still been turning up. We have also noticed changes in attitudes and the offenders themselves have said that they have made changes in their lifestyles.

The black clients that we have on the programme seem to do much, much better than the white clients we have here. Completion rates seem to improve with black men who have been on the programme. Self-reports from black men show that they have a better experience going through the programme. They have enhanced self-confidence.

Interviewees generally felt that an important aspect in the success of programmes was that participants had the opportunity to discuss their offending behaviour with other offenders and facilitators of the same ethnic background. This environment allowed offenders to share their experiences of racism with others who would be able to empathise. They generally agreed that the facilitators and invited speakers acted as good role models that the offenders could identify with.

Some staff noted that where a number of different cultures were represented within a group, the opportunity arose for offenders to share aspects of their culture and religion with group members. This was sometimes considered to be an empowering and confidence-building experience. It also allowed others to reflect on how this compared with their own culture and experiences.

Teaching black history was also considered to be a positive aspect of the programmes that usually received good feedback from those attending. Again this was considered to be a confidence-building exercise. Understanding the offenders' culture was considered to be important, so facilitators could help to identify when the offender was likely to be in a high-risk situation for reoffending. Some of these successful aspects of the programmes are illustrated in the quote below:

Specific elements that make the programme work are offering them the opportunity to discuss the issues that they have to face in everyday life, in terms of growing up, talk about racism and how it affects their behaviour. And making sure the environment is one where they feel able to share that information with each other and us as officers. Also making sure that they feel that they can be respected as individuals, that their views do count and, most importantly, that they are heard.

All staff interviewed believed that there were strong links between the offending behaviour of black and Asian offenders and their experiences of racism. The experiences of black and Asian offenders were suggested, by those interviewed, as being distinct from white offenders in terms of their experiences of racism, especially institutional racism, which affected their educational and employment opportunities as well as how they had been treated within the criminal justice system. Interviewees felt that specialist provision for minority ethnic offenders was needed to address these issues because tackling the impact of racism on behaviour was very difficult in groups where the majority is white. They thought that white offenders' lack of understanding of issues that may arise out of experiences of racism made them more likely to be dismissive of the impact of racism.

> [Black and Asian offenders] *have had very different experiences to white offenders and because of this, the groups become very different. Experiences such as racism, for example, finding it harder to get employment, constantly being stopped by the police, black offenders regard these experiences as the norm. Trying to tackle these issues in a mixed group is much harder because white offenders will have no understanding of these experiences and will be more dismissive of these issues. In a black group you can give time and space to look at these issues and how they then impact on behaviour.*

Programme deliverers also thought that because many black and Asian offenders had had disadvantaged access to education and employment, it was important to incorporate sessions aimed at assisting offenders to find employment and suitable training courses.

> *Racism has a negative impact on black offenders, which affects their prospects in the education and employment areas and has an impact on their experience of the criminal justice system. The programme teaches them skills to cope with these experiences of racism. Race is a static factor; in other words it will never go away. It is often a contributing factor in a black person's offending.*

Evaluations of individual programmes

In addition to the very positive views of staff involved in developing and delivering programmes, four initiatives had been evaluated to look at the outcomes for offenders. Although these are based on very small numbers of individuals, and only two include any measure of reoffending by programme participants, their findings are very encouraging.

One of the studies used psychometric tests to measure changes in offenders' attitudes over the course of the programme. However, many of the programmes reported difficulty conducting psychometric tests on offenders because they felt that there was a lack of appropriate tests available that measure change for black and Asian offenders. Two services were so dissatisfied with existing psychometric tests that they had decided to develop their own tests. Both were still under development at the time of interview.

Black Offending Behaviour Programme, Greater Manchester Probation Service

This evaluation involved questionnaires and interviews with staff delivering the programme. It interviewed a small number of offenders (six completers, four non-completers) both before and after the programme completion and measured changes in psychometric test scores over the course of the programme. Overall, the feedback from both offenders and staff involved in the programme was positive. They felt that it met the aims and objectives of the black empowerment module very well and that the programme as a whole was very useful for black offenders.

Changes in some of the psychometric test scores also showed changes in a positive direction at the end of the programme. Findings from Crime Pics II[22] suggested that the programme had an impact on the attitudes of offenders with regard to their general attitude to reoffending, anticipation of reoffending and denial of victim hurt (Williams, 2001). However, this study did not examine whether positive offender feedback and changes in psychometric test scores were followed by a change in offending behaviour.

Greenwich and Lewisham Black Self-Development and Educational Attainment Group, Inner London Probation Service

This study involved unstructured interviews with group-work officers and group interviews with offenders. The programmes had a good completion rate: 15 of the 22 people starting one of the three groups completed all the sessions. The percentage of completers increased as the courses ran so that the final course achieved a 100 per cent completion rate despite the demands on individuals' time being higher than in the majority of group-work programmes. Offenders' feedback was very positive. Being in an all black group was, for many participants, a new experience that they found valuable and safe. Feedback generally suggested that offenders were able to use the self-development materials to fundamentally question their previous behaviour and develop new ways of coping with pressures (Durrance et al., 2001).

---

22. Crime Pics II is a psychometirc test that consists of five subscales: the general attitude toward reoffending, anticipation of reoffending, victim hurt denial, evaluation of crime as a worthwhile lifestyle and perception of current life problems.

Black Self-Development Programme, Inner London Probation Service

The Black Self-Development Programme compared reconviction rates of offenders attending two of the programmes with white offenders completing a comparable programme. Those completing the programme had considerably lower reconviction rates than white offenders: 51 per cent (18/35) of black offenders were reconvicted within two years of completing the programme compared to 75 per cent (38/51) of white offenders. This is despite risk of reconviction scores (as measured using OGRS) being higher for black offenders (Durrance *et al.*, 2001).

Black People and Offending Programme, West Midlands Probation Service

A small reconviction study was also conducted on two groups of offenders completing this black people and offending programme. It was based on 13 offenders, eight of whom completed the programme. This found that the actual reconviction rates were much lower than those predicted two years after completing the programme: 25 per cent of completers were reconvicted compared to a predicted rate of 50 per cent (using OGRS2). Sixty per cent of non-completers were reconvicted compared to a predicted rate of 48 per cent (Dunn, 2000).

Conclusion

While the views of staff involved in developing or delivering the programmes and results of the four evaluations conducted to date are very encouraging, it is difficult to draw a firm conclusion about the effectiveness of the programmes on the basis of the evidence available currently. Methodological difficulties, small sample sizes, use of appropriate psychometric tests and limited long-term reconviction data, mean that findings from the evaluations cannot been seen as conclusive. Also, little research has considered the views of offenders themselves and these might be different from those of probation staff. There are a number of on-going research studies that will provide a great deal of information both about the needs of black and Asian offenders and their experience of probation[23] and also outcomes for black and Asian offenders doing accredited offending programmes[24]. These will tell us more about the criminogenic needs of minority ethnic offenders and the impact that racism and marginalisation has upon their behaviour.

---

23. The Home Office has commissioned a team from the Universities of Glamorgan, Lancaster, Lincolnshire and Wales at Swansea led by Dr Ali Wardak to conduct a survey of 500 black and Asian men on probation. This will explore their experience of probation supervision and also their criminogenic needs.
24. A number of studies are currently looking at outcomes for offenders doing various accredited and non-accredited offending programmes including a study of Think First by the Probation Studies Unit, Oxford University and a study of seven different programmes by Leicester and Liverpool Universities.

5.   Conclusion

This study was commissioned to fill a gap in our knowledge of effective work with black and Asian offenders. Only five programmes were identified as currently running in the 45 Probation Services that responded to a survey. A further seven had been developed but were not currently running. Interviews with staff responsible for either developing or delivering the programmes found that all strongly believed that separate specialist provision is essential for most minority ethnic offenders. The findings of evaluations that have looked at outcomes for four of the programmes are encouraging but methodological problems, not least the small numbers of participants, make it difficult to draw definitive conclusions.

Therefore this study has been able to describe a number of programmes that have been developed for black and Asian offenders and identify factors that those either developing or delivering the programmes thought were vital to their success or failure. However, it cannot establish if black and Asian offenders have specific criminogenic needs that are distinct from those of white offenders on the basis of the currently available evidence. It also cannot say whether black and Asian offenders are more effectively provided for through separate probation programmes or whether their needs can be met in mixed race groups. It is clear, however, that it is important to avoid black and Asian offenders being isolated and marginalised in groups by ensuring that they are not allocated to programmes where they make up only a small proportion of offenders. A practical implication of this is that it may not possible for black and Asian offenders to participate in groups in some areas where very small numbers of black and Asian offenders are supervised at any one time. Here it will be important that special measures are put into place so that black and Asian offenders can benefit from group-work. This may mean having specialists to deliver one-to-one programmes with offenders or offering additional support (e.g. mentors) to offenders doing programmes in mixed race groups.

The factors that programme developers and deliverers considered to be vital to the success of programmes for black and Asian offenders are listed below. Some apply more generally to group-work programmes and are not restricted to work with black and Asian offenders.

Whole service commitment to programme

Programmes are more likely to remain in operation if they are seen as an integral part of service provision and are given the same status as other offending behaviour programmes. To date, interventions have been more likely to survive where they were implemented in a large metropolitan area as part of a service-wide initiative. This ensured sufficient numbers of black and Asian offenders to attend programmes because referrals were received from across the whole service. Programmes that had been implemented as part of a service initiative rather than set up by a few dedicated members of staff also had better training for all probation staff in working with black and Asian offenders. Training increased all staffs' awareness of the benefits of black and Asian offender programmes and so led to higher referral rates.

Management support

Management support was vital to successful implementation and the continuation of groups. Programme developers and deliverers cited this as the main reason for programmes finishing. However, few managers' views were sought. The types of support that staff discussed were:

- adequate time and work load relief to develop programmes and prepare for sessions;
- training for facilitators in delivering programmes and dealing with issues that arise; and
- adequate resources for programmes to be set up and delivered. This included having interpreters available, having culturally relevant materials and being able to 'buy-in' the services of academic consultants and outside speakers.

Characteristics of facilitators/group leaders

Having committed and competent facilitators with a good understanding of black and Asian offenders was important to the success of programmes. Programme tutors needed to be able to engage the offenders, show empathy and have a good understanding of their culture and the impact of racism on their behaviour. It was generally agreed that facilitators should be from a minority ethnic background but this can be difficult for programmes aimed at Asian offenders, as Asians are under-represented in the Probation Service. Further research could usefully examine the recruitment and retention of minority ethnic officers to group-work positions, for example, by interviewing a sample of previous and present black and Asian probation officers to find out their experiences of working in the service. This study should also seek the views of those in management positions with responsibility for staff recruitment.

It was also important to have a gender balance of facilitators both to stop facilitators colluding with groups made up mainly of men and also to support women in the groups. Some programmes were very dependent upon key staff and areas should actively seek to replace tutors who leave.

External experts

Programmes can make use of external experts in several ways:

- *To develop the programmes.* Programmes that employed external experts at the developmental stage to advise on programme theory and contents were more likely to be successfully developed and implemented;
- *To evaluate the programmes.* Academics could also be used to evaluate programmes and establish monitoring systems, especially where there is no in-house research capacity;
- *As mentors.* Many programmes invite successful professionals and business people to speak to the group and act as role models. Some also assign mentors of a similar ethnic background to the offenders to support them during the programme and subsequently. However, mentoring schemes must be properly organised and require an identified member of staff to take responsibility for their implementation and be given adequate time and resources to do this; and
- *As speakers.* Groups can also invite speakers from agencies working with black and Asian communities (e.g. specialist housing providers) or from agencies that offenders might use (e.g. health or drug agencies). These speakers can both inform the offenders and be seen as positive role models.

Programme model and theory

Programme developers and deliverers believed that interventions for black and Asian offenders should include a range of issues, not just black empowerment. Programmes that were most likely to survive and reported to have the greater success in changing attitudes and behaviour were those that also addressed offending behaviour and education, employment and training. Those that addressed a specific offence type were reported to be successful when they adapted an existing programme to make it culturally relevant.

Those with experience of developing or delivering programmes thought that it was important to use a 'holistic approach' in work with black and Asian offenders, especially as there is no strong evidence base that a single approach works best with this group. Cognitive-behavioural and pro-social modelling approaches were considered by those interviewed to be effective with black and Asian offenders.

Programme intensity

Longer and more intensive programmes were considered to engage participants more effectively, increase attendance and have a greater impact on the offenders' subsequent behaviour. Generally, probation supervision is increasingly incorporating a number of interventions based on an assessment of need. Not all black and Asian offenders will be assessed as having a need for this type of programme. It is important to recognise that there is a potential risk of unequal treatment for black and Asian offenders who attend modules 'added on' to accredited general offending behaviour programmes as they will, in practice, be subject to more intensive supervision than comparable white offenders. It is important that future research examines carefully the relationship between length of programmes and completion and breach rates to make sure that black and Asian offenders are not disadvantaged.

Active participation

An active participation learning style was reported to work best. This includes discussions, role-plays and encouraging all participants to share their experiences with the group and teach the group about their own culture. This style has been found to be the most effective with offenders more generally (Vennard and Hedderman, 1998).

Programme integrity

All probation programmes are being encouraged to implement measures to ensure programme integrity and this equally applies to work with black and Asian offenders. The programmes that were currently running had generally begun to address this issue by video recording sessions and/or completing integrity checklists.

Case management

Good liaison is needed between supervising officers and programme deliverers if supervising officers are going to build upon the offender's experience of the programme. Supervising officers need to understand the programme's aims and contents and course tutors need to tell supervising officers of any arising issues so they are able to organise follow-on work. The best way of doing this is a problem facing all offending behaviour programmes. For this to be most effective the systems for liaison should be formalised and monitored. Time should also be allocated for this to take place.

Good referral systems

A major reason why some interventions did not continue was that they received a small number of referrals. Areas need to establish formal referral systems rather than relying on facilitators seeking out referrals as sometimes happened in the past. Programmes must be well advertised and probation staff and sentencers need to understand the aims and contents of the intervention.

Effective targeting

Generally, programmes underpinned by 'What Works' principles have specific targeting criteria for offenders. In this study, those programmes currently running had stricter targeting criteria than those that had previously folded. Simply being black or Asian was not sufficient reason to do the programme. Targeting criteria could include a range of factors e.g. risk category, sex, whether offending may be related to experiences of racism and whether the offender is able to demonstrate a motivation to change. Offence type may be relevant for some programmes. Age was not considered to be important; in fact having a wide range of ages was seen as beneficial.

It is important to consider if programmes should be targeted according to race. Where participants are from a range of ethnic backgrounds, it is important to ensure their needs can be met within the group and that no one will feel marginalised. This may be a particular issue where Asian offenders form a minority in groups made up mainly of black offenders, as there is a relatively small number of Asian offenders under probation supervision. Programme facilitators, mentors and invited speakers should also be selected so they are representative of the ethnic make-up of the group.

Building an evidence base

Finally, systems should be put into place to evaluate the effectiveness of programmes using either in-house research units or outside consultants. Again this applies to all programmes, not just those for black and Asian offenders. Evaluations need to have a robust design and include a sufficient number of offenders to produce meaningful results. They might use feedback from staff and offenders, outcomes at the end of programmes including changes in attitudes measured by psychometric tests, and an analysis of reconviction rates. Where possible, outcomes for black and Asian offenders in separate groups should be compared against those for white offenders receiving comparable interventions and/or black and Asian offenders attending similar programmes in mixed race groups. Ideally, some measure of the cost of programmes and cost-effectiveness should be conducted.

Two other research studies will also inform the development of future probation work. Firstly, the Home Office has commissioned a survey of 500 black and Asian men on probation. This will examine both their criminogenic needs and their experiences of probation provision. It will also explore the views of offenders with regard to what might work to help them desist from offending behaviour. The study will be completed in 2003. Secondly, the National Probation Directorate has identified five models of working with black and Asian offenders that will be tested in various areas in England and Wales. The study begins at the end of 2002 and will last for two and half years. The five models are:

- Delivery of a black self-development module followed by a general offending behaviour programme to black and Asian offenders;
- Delivery of a black self-development module to black and Asian offenders followed by attendance on a general offending behaviour programme delivered to mixed groups;
- Delivery of a black self-development module plus a reintegration module (e.g. employment);
- Delivery of a mixed general offending programme with mentoring for black and Asian offenders; and
- Delivery of Accredited Drink Impaired Drivers programme to Asian offenders.

The evaluations of these models will, together with the other research outlined above, build upon this study to fill the gaps in our knowledge about 'What Works' with black and Asian offenders on probation.

Appendix 1   Case studies

Those responsible for developing or delivering programmes for ten of the 13 groups identified in the survey were interviewed. The interviews covered a range of topics including:

- Personal data about the interviewees;
- History of the intervention's development e.g. how its was developed, length of development, staff involved and its underlying theoretical basis (if any);
- Profile of the group's participants – e.g. age, gender, ethnicity and most common offence;
- Profile of the group – e.g. throughput, drop-out rates, staff to offender ratio, targeting criteria;
- Referral procedures and number of referrals;
- Content of the intervention e.g. theory model, targets for change, organisation of the programme, topics covered, learning style and course materials. Also number, frequency and duration of sessions, when sessions are run, and whether the programme is run according to demand;
- Case management arrangements and any provision for follow-on work;
- Personnel and administrative issues e.g. numbers and grades of programme deliverers, staffs' training, management support and accommodation;
- Monitoring and evaluation arrangements and results (if any); and
- Interviewees' views about what works with black and Asian offenders. This included factors contributing to the programme's success (or failure) and their views on the importance of separate and/or specialist provision for black and Asian offenders and their criminogenic needs.

Current programmes

1. Black Offending Behaviour Programme, *Greater Manchester Probation Service*
Interview conducted July 2000

This combines a black self-development module with the Think First general offending programme. There is an induction session and four sessions on black self-development prior to the Think First programme (21 sessions). A mentoring component runs alongside the group-work sessions. Sessions are run in the evenings. It is generally a closed programme.

The black offending programme has been running since May 2000 and replaced the New Directions Programme previously run in the service. It was developed over 12 months (from May 1999) and external academic consultants were involved in the development process and staff training.

Profile of the group
Participants are men, aged 17 plus. It is open to those who identify themselves as 'black' (the definition from the Black Workers Forum was used which defines 'black' as people of African/Caribbean or Asian origin and other descents who have a common experience of racism and discrimination). Attendance on the course was optional and eligibility was identified in a face-to-face assessment. The offender must have three or more convictions, but in practice most have more (mean = 20). They must be at risk of further offending, must acknowledge some responsibility for current offences and must demonstrate some motivation to change behaviour and attend the programme. The programme is a condition of either a community sentence or post-release licence. Although the programme was designed for medium to high-risk offenders, those who have attended the programme have generally been high-risk offenders (mean OGRS score of 81.25 (Range 41-94)). The high-risk score means that many would fall outside the Think First eligibility band.

Numbers of offenders on the programme range from four to 12. Programme deliverers reported low drop-out rates.

Profile of the programme
The programme is based on cognitive-behavioural theory and also includes an educational component and a black empowerment module. Topics covered in the empowerment module include self-identity, racism, discrimination, black achievements, how black people devalue themselves, citizenship and similarities. It aims to help group members identify the impact of racism on their life experiences, including offending behaviour. Sessions explore levels and types of internalised, externalised and institutional racism and assist the offenders in developing strategies to address the impact of racism. The aim of the Think First module is to assist in the reduction of reoffending by using cognitive-behavioural methods. The programme is fully documented and has a theory manual. All sessions are videotaped to examine programme integrity.

Two probation officers deliver the programme. Additionally, four mentors have been recruited from community-based agencies (both South Asian and African/Caribbean community initiatives). Mentors attend pre-programme meetings and meetings with case managers as well as group-work sessions.

Monitoring and evaluation
An evaluation officer has been appointed specifically to evaluate the programme and is advised by an external academic consultant. The evaluation covers profiles of group participants, offender feedback, programme deliverer and case-manager feedback, and comparison of psychometric test scores pre and post intervention (Williams, 2001). The report of the evaluation is discussed in Chapter 4.

2. The Greenwich and Lewisham Black Self-Development and Educational Attainment Group,
Inner London Probation Service (ILPS) Interview conducted in August 2000

This integrates black empowerment work with offending behaviour work and sessions of education, training and employment. It has been running in the South East consortia of ILPS since the beginning of 1999 and was extended across central London in 2000.

Development of the group
The programme was in development for 18 months prior to 1999 and was piloted over a six-month period. It was developed by four probation officers, an external academic consultant and a team of employment, training and education providers who commissioned an education, training and employment (ETE) course for black offenders that forms part of the current programme. The ETE programme was accredited by the London Open College Network.

Profile of participants
Participants are mainly men of African/Caribbean culture. No Asians had started the course at time of interview (August 2000) and only five women had completed the programme. The average (mean) age of group members is 25 years (range 18-38). Participants tend to be low to medium-risk offenders, with a mean OGRS score of 54 per cent (ranges from 17% to 98%). Offenders are also assessed on their suitability for the programme.

Profile of the programme
The programme is based on a combination of theoretical models: cognitive behavioural, educational, control theory, the development of black self-identity and the wider social perspective. Topics covered include black history, the impact of institutionalised racism, decision-making and choices, skills and knowledge, changing behaviours and attitudes, relationships, writing a CV and interpreting job descriptions and person specifications, preparing for interviews and making constructive career and lifestyle choices.

The programme is 20 three-hour sessions delivered in the daytime over a ten-week period. It is run regularly and is a closed programme. Three probation officers are responsible for the offending and black awareness sessions while an education, training and employment (ETE) trainer has responsibility for delivering the education, training and employment sessions. A number of partnership agencies provide guest speakers that may include business men and women, consultants and teachers. All speakers have the same cultural background as the offenders to facilitate community reintegration and pro-social modelling. The programme is fully documented in a manual (including an introduction to the theoretical basis).

Profile of the group
Group sizes range from six to eight offenders. Low drop-out rates were reported for the programme and the most recent course had achieved a 100 per cent completion rate. Overall the completion rate is 68 per cent, which is higher than that achieved on many other offending behaviour programmes run by the service.

Evaluation and monitoring
Good evaluative work has been conducted on the programme and a full report of the evaluation exists (Durrance *et al.*, 2001). The evaluation includes participant profiles, drop-out rates, programme integrity and views of participants and staff towards the course. ILPS are currently developing a psychometric test that can be used to assist in the evaluation of the programme. Reconviction data are not included, as the programme has not been running for a sufficient length of time for such data to be meaningful. The findings of the evaluation are discussed in Chapter 4.

3. Black Self-Development (component of R&R), *Inner London Probation Service (ILPS)*
Interview conducted in September 2000

This is a module undertaken in addition to the Reasoning and Rehabilitation (R&R) general offending programme as well as education, training and employment (ETE) sessions. The R&R programme and ETE sessions are delivered in mixed ethnicity groups.

History of the programme
The Black Self-Development Group has been in existence since 1992. It is delivered at Camberwell Probation Centre and Sherbourne House but is open to black offenders across the whole of ILPS. The programme developers employed an external consultant to assist in the development of the programme.

Profile of participants
Participants are men, mostly of African/Caribbean, Pakistani and Bangladeshi origin. Ages range from 21 to 65 but most tend to be between 20 and 30. The programme is open to more serious or persistent offenders, with an OGRS score of 75 or over.

Profile of the programme
The programme is 12, two-hour sessions run during daytime. It is an intensive, closed programme. It draws on several theory models including cognitive behavioural, educational and black psychology theories. Topics covered include black history, black culture, internalised racism, values, and relationships. The programme is fully documented in a course manual. Four probation officers deliver the programme who are recruited specifically for their ability to run it.

Profile of the group
The average number of participants in a group is five, with the numbers ranging from four to ten. Completion rates appear to be higher for black men who have attended the programme than for white offenders attending a similar programme.

Monitoring and evaluation
The programme has been evaluated (Durrance *et al.*, 2000). See Chapter 4 for a discussion of the evaluation.

4. Black Probation Group, *South East London Probation Service*
Interview conducted in August 2000

The programme is based on black empowerment and follows a cognitive-behavioural model. Topics covered include assertiveness and communication, enhancing personal responsibility, alternative thinking, goal setting, victim empathy and problem solving.

History of the programme
The Black Probation Group has been running for over ten years. The impetus for its development came from black probation officers who recognised a gap in service provision. The programme was developed over an 18-month period and employed an anti-racist consultant to assist in the development process.

Profile of participants
The group is targeted at 'black' offenders (most of whom are African/Caribbean) aged 18 plus. Participants are not targeted by offence type or level of risk. Most participants are

men, only two women have completed the programme. On average, 12 offenders start the programme and seven complete. Drop-out rates are comparable with other offending behaviour programmes run in south-east London.

Profile of the programme
The programme is ten sessions lasting 90 minutes each, although it is planned to expand to 12 sessions. It is delivered in the evening by two or three probation officers. The programme contents are fully documented in the course handbook. It has been difficult to recruit appropriate staff and so some sessions have been run by mainstream officers rather than specialists in group-work.

Monitoring and evaluation
It has not yet been formally evaluated but South East London Probation Service was planning to evaluate it in the future.

5. Black People and Offending, *West Midlands Probation Service*
Interview conducted in October 2000

This follows a cognitive-behavioural approach but also makes use of empowerment and social learning theory to address internalised racism. Topics covered include: self-affirmation and development, black crimes, learning, communication and thinking, victim perspective, role models, reforming attitudes, drug abuse, violence and aggression and maintaining offending-free lifestyle.

History of the programme
It has been running since January 1996. It currently only runs in the Birmingham area but it is planned to roll it out across the region. The programme is currently being revised.

Profile of participants
Participants are men aged 17 and over. Most are African/Caribbean, with some Asian offenders. Participants are medium to high-risk offenders who are being diverted away from custody.

Profile of the programme
The programme is currently eight, two-hour sessions. (The revised version will be 12 two-hour sessions.) Sessions are generally run during the day, but evening provision is also available. It is a closed programme. The average number starting a group is eight. Three or four participants usually drop out before the end.

Currently, groups are facilitated by two probation officers. The service is exploring the feasibility of using mentors of the same ethnic background as participants in the revised programme. It is also writing a theory manual for the new programme and exploring suitable psychometric tests. Facilitators are considering developing a test specifically for this programme.

Monitoring and evaluation
Internal evaluations have been conducted on each of the programmes delivered which have reported positive feedback from the participants and their supervising officers. A small-scale reconviction study also indicated positive results (Dunn, 2000). This is reported in Chapter 4.

Programmes no longer running

6. Asian Alcohol Impaired Drivers, *Leicestershire and Rutland Probation Service*
Interview conducted in November 2000

It was based on an existing drink-drive programme that was adapted to make it culturally relevant. The programme used both cognitive-behavioural and educational models.

History of the programme
This was set up in 1992. Although the service has not officially ended the programme, no courses have been delivered since the end of 1998 because there is a shortage of available staff to run the programme, a lack of referrals and a reported lack of management commitment. The initiative to develop the programme came from a probation officer who identified a need for such a programme. Service management also supported it.

Profile of participants
The group was targeted at Asian men with at least one drink-driving conviction. They were aged 17 years or over, with the majority being 30 to 40. Most men who attended were Sikh.

Profile of the programme
The programme was delivered once a week during the evenings. It lasted for six, two-hour sessions. It was an open programme, with offenders able to join at any point and ran regularly. Two Asian probation officers and an Asian volunteer delivered the programme. Translators were employed to assist those offenders who had poor English skills. Group participants would also assist those with poor English. An Asian representative from Alcoholics Anonymous and an Asian alcohol counsellor were invited to come and speak to the participants. An Asian female also spoke to the group on the effects of alcohol abuse on significant others.

The average number of offenders on the programmes was ten. Drop-out rates were reported to be very low, with many of the programmes experiencing no drop-out from offenders. However, it was not running at the time of interview because of the lack of available, motivated staff to facilitate.

Monitoring and evaluation
No formal evaluation has been carried out of this programme.

7. Group for Asian Drink Drivers, *West Midlands Probation Service*
Interviews conducted in November and December 2000

The programme incorporated the principles of a number of theories including cognitive-behavioural and educational.

History of the programme
This ran from 1995 to 1997 in West Midlands Probation Service. Programme development began in 1994 after probation staff identified a need for such a programme and management agreed to its development.

Profile of participants
Participants were men, aged 18 or over, of Asian culture and high-risk drink drivers. Most were Sikh.

Profile of the programme
It consisted of six, two-hour sessions and was delivered both during daytime and evenings. It was a closed programme. It was delivered by two probation officers, both of whom were Asian. Offenders were referred on to the programme by probation officers at PSR stage.

The numbers in each group ranged from six to eight offenders. Drop-out rates were reported to be very low. The first programme began with six participants, none of whom dropped out. The programme folded due to lack of management support and resources.

Monitoring and evaluation
No formal evaluation was conducted of the programme.

8. Black Offender Programme, *West Yorkshire Probation Service*
Interview conducted in September 2000

This focused on offending behaviour and black empowerment and made use of mentors. It incorporated several different theories including cognitive-behavioural, educational, control theory and black empowerment. Topics covered included social skills training, addressing offending behaviour, black history, black culture and coping with racism.

History of the programme
This programme was developed in West Yorkshire between 1994 and 1995 by five probation officers within the area with a special interest in provision for black offenders. A pilot programme ran in 1995 but it was not developed further. They consulted an American psychologist about 'black psychology' and the contents of the programme.

Profile of participants
Participants were African/Caribbean and Asian men between 23 and 33 years of age. They were medium to high-risk, persistent offenders.

Profile of the programme
The programme was fairly intensive, consisting of 16 sessions, running over 3.5 days a week. It was a closed programme. Three probation officers and one Probation Service officer delivered it. A number of black professionals including a black drugs worker, a black barrister and an Asian barrister were invited to speak to the group.

Six offenders began the programme and all completed. The programme did not develop into an integral programme within West Yorkshire Probation Service. Staff involved in the development and delivery of the intervention felt that it was undermined because some of the larger divisions within the service were not committed to the programme. Also, they felt there was a reluctance or refusal by magistrates to make orders with the necessary conditions to attend the programme.

Monitoring and evaluation
No formal evaluation was conducted of the programme.

9. Face the Future Programme, *West Yorkshire Probation Service*
Interview conducted in September 2000

This was based on the generic 'Face the Future' general offending behaviour programme that was being delivered in West Yorkshire and was adapted to be more culturally relevant to black offenders. The Face the Future programme has a cognitive-behavioural theory base and focuses upon the offending behaviour of the participants. The programme for black and Asian offenders also covered issues of racism and how to deal with this, awareness and empowerment. It also included educational elements.

History of the programme
This was established in West Yorkshire in 1996. Four programmes were delivered, but it was no longer running.

Profile of participants
Participants were African/Caribbean or Asian men aged 19 and 44 (average age = early 20s). They were medium to high-risk offenders with a history of offending and who were at risk of receiving a custodial sentence.

Profile of the programme
The course was divided into modules delivered over a five-week period for 3.5 days a week. It was held during the daytime and was a closed programme. It was delivered by three probation officers. Mentors were invited to the sessions to speak to the offenders on such issues as training and employment. The service experienced some problems recruiting black probation officers to run the intervention, as some staff felt there should have been a greater focus on culture rather than offending.

The average number of offenders in a group was eight. Drop-out rates were reported to be lower for this programme than those for white offenders. Programme deliverers reported that managers decided to end the programme because they felt the programme was expensive and resources would be better placed elsewhere.

Monitoring and evaluation
No monitoring or evaluation was undertaken.

10. Black Empowerment Group, *Hereford and Worcester Probation Service*
Interview conducted in July 2000

This drew on educational, cognitive-behavioural, social action and empowerment theories. Topics covered included being black in Britain today, problem solving, personal empowerment, education and training.

History of the programme
One Black Empowerment Group was run in March 2000. The same programme has been running in prisons since 1997 and had been developed jointly by the Prison and Probation Service. It was due to be delivered in the community in 1998 but was delayed by lack of referrals and resources.

Profile of participants
Participants were black and Asian offenders aged 18 or over. They were nearly all men (only one woman attended the course). Although the programme did not specify offence level of risk, participants tended to be low-risk offenders.

Profile of the programme
It was made up of four, two-hour sessions delivered weekly in the evenings. The programme was closed. Two probation staff delivered the course. Six offenders were referred to the programme and four actually attended.

Monitoring and evaluation
No formal evaluation was conducted on the programme although participants' feedback was collected.

11. New Directions Groupwork Programme, *Greater Manchester Probation Service*
Interview conducted in July 2000

This programme was based on cognitive-behavioural theory. The approach it took was information and advice giving, victim awareness and empathy skills, social cause and effect, reasoning skills and other cognitive skills including decision-making and alternate thinking. It was not exclusively for black and Asian offenders but in practice only ten per cent of participants were white (4/42).

History of the programme
This ran six times between 1994 and 1996. It was originally developed because of the high number of drug-related offences occurring in a particular area of Manchester. Development work began in 1992. It was no longer running because the main course deliverer left and this post was never filled, due to resourcing problems. Also it was felt that it was no longer sufficient because developments in group-work provision meant that programmes were expected to place greater emphasis on theoretical models, be evidence based and area initiatives.

Programme participants
The offenders attending the programme were mainly men aged 25 to 35. Only one woman attended the course. It was not exclusively for black offenders but most were from minority ethnic backgrounds. (Of the 42 offenders attending, four were white, 35 black and three Asian.) All had convictions for offences related to the supply of drugs.

Profile of the programme
The length of the programme varied between four and eight two-hour sessions delivered once a week. It was delivered by two or three probation officers. On average seven offenders attended the course.

Monitoring and evaluation
An evaluation conducted in 1997 looked at the views of those involved retrospectively. It showed positive responses from participants and programme deliverers.

Programmes that did not run

12. Empowerment Programme for Black Probationers and Licensees, *Merseyside Probation Service* Interview conducted in October 2000

This covered topics including experience of racism and how to deal with such experiences, resources available and how to access these, issues around stereotyping and positive role models, empowerment and how to improve employability. It never ran.

History of the programme
This was developed in Merseyside Probation Service during 1998. The initiative for it came from a working group who identified a need for such a programme. Development was undertaken by a multi-disciplinary team including the Probation Service, a skills agency, the police and the local authority. The programme was never delivered because the facilitators did not receive any referrals. The reason offered for the lack of referrals was because all the offenders approached to attend the programme declined the opportunity to attend.

Programme participants
The programme was aimed at black offenders on probation orders or licence who volunteered to participate.

Profile of the programme
It was designed to take place over three consecutive, full days.

Appendix 2

Theoretical approaches used in programmes for black and Asian offenders

Cognitive-behavioural

Cognitive-behavioural techniques are mainly developed from social learning theory which understands behaviour to be the result of learning experiences encountered in the course of growing up, either directly or through observational learning. As an approach to working with offenders, cognitive-behavioural modification assumes that offenders are shaped by their environment and have failed to acquire certain cognitive skills or have learnt inappropriate ways of behaving. Offender programmes based on this premise are intended to teach offenders to face up to what they have done, understand their motives and develop new coping strategies and ways of controlling their behaviour.

Control theory

Control theory involves the investigation of the controls that keep the behaviour of most people within the law. These can be external controls such as the existence of reasonable limits and significant supportive relationships, but can also be internal controls such as a strong self-concept as a law-abiding person or a high frustration tolerance on the realisation that different opportunities are available to different groups. In the case of black offenders is has been suggested that exposure to racism can damage the black person's conception of themselves and that this can have implications for their behaviour. Programmes that base themselves on this theory may attempt to develop these controls with the aim of influencing an individual's propensity to offend.

Education

It is believed that institutional racism experienced by minority ethnic groups leads to their being disadvantaged in the education system and labour market, resulting in poorer academic performance and difficulties in securing employment. Low educational achievement and unemployment have both been related to offending behaviour. Programmes for offenders may offer education aimed at improving things such as basic skills, literacy, numeracy and employment skills.

Empowerment

Some programmes for black and Asian offenders are based on the belief that offending behaviour among this group is the result of experiences of racism. These tend to offer strategies for empowerment that aim to give offenders the ability to tackle racism which they face in daily life without resorting to crime.

Akhtar, S. (2001). *An evaluation of the Prison Service Sex Offender Treatment Programme, Enhanced Thinking Skills Programme, Reasoning and Rehabilitation Programme. To see if the treatment needs of black offenders are being met.* Unpublished report.

Andrews, D.A. (1995). The psychology of criminal conduct and effective treatment. In J. McGuire (ed.) *What Works? Reducing Reoffending.* Chichester: Wiley.

Bagihole, B. (1997). *Equal Opportunities and Social Policy.* London: Longman.

Barker, M., Geraghty, J., Webb, B., and Key, T. (1993). *The Prevention of Street Robbery.* Police Research Group Crime Prevention Series Paper No.44. London: Home Office.

Bowling, B. and Phillips, C. (2002). *Racism, Crime and Justice.* London: Longman Criminology Series.

Bowling, B. (1991). 'Ethnic minority elderly people: helping the community to care.' *New Community* 17(4): 645-652.

Brown, D. and Poole, L. (1997). *Evaluation of the New Directions Groupwork Programme. Draft.* Manchester: Greater Manchester Probation Service.

Briggs, C. (1995). 'Policing Moss Side: A Probation Response'. *Probation Journal* June 1995 pp. 62-66.

Briggs, C. (1996). 'The Community Strikes Back'. *Criminal Justice. The magazine of the Howard League* 14 (2) pp.15.

Caddick, B. (1993). 'Using Groups in Working with Offenders: a Survey of Groupwork in the Probation Services of England and Wales'. In Brown, A. and Caddick, B.(Eds.) *Groupwork with Offenders.* London: Whiting and Birch.

Central Council of Probation Committees Steering Group on Inner Cities. (1983). *Probation a multi-racial approach.* London: Central Council of Probation Committees.

Commission for Racial Equality. (1996). *Exclusion from School. The Public Cost.* London: Commission for Racial Equality.

Coombe, V. (1986). *Race and social work: a guide to training.* London: Tavistock.

Day, M., Hall, T. and Griffiths, C. (1989). *Black people and the criminal justice system: three speeches given at the Howard League Conference on 'Minorities, Crime and Justice'.* London: The Howard League for Penal Reform.

Denney, D. (1992). *Racism and Anti-Racism in Probation.* London: Routledge.

Department for Education and Employment. (2001a). *Youth Cohort Study: The Activities and Experiences of 16 year olds: England and Wales. 2000.* London, DfEE.

Department for Education and Employment. (2001b). *Youth Cohort Study: The Activities and Experiences of 18 year olds: England and Wales. 2000.* London, DfEE.

Department of the Environment, Transport and the Regions. (2000). 1999/00 *Survey of English Housing: Preliminary results.* Housing Statistics Summary No.7. [www.housing.detr.gov.uk/research/seh/]

Dominelli, L., Jeffers, L., Jones, G., Sibanda, S. and Williams, B. (1995). *Anti-Racist Probation Practice.* Aldershot: Arena.

Dunn, M. (2000). *Recidivism Report of the Black Offender Group Pilots.* West Midlands Probation Service.

Durrance, P., Hignett, C., Merone, L. and Asamoah, A. (2001). *The Greenwich and Lewisham Black Self-Development and Educational Attainment Group Evaluation Report.* Inner London Probation Service.

Farrington, D.P. (1997). 'Human Development and Criminal Careers' In Maguire, M. *et al.* (Eds.) *The Oxford Handbook of Criminology.* Oxford: Clarendon Press.

Farrington, D.P. (1996). *Understanding and Preventing Youth Crime.* Joseph Rowntree Foundation: York.

Fisher, K. and Watkins, L. (1993). 'Inside Groupwork' in Brown, A. and Caddick, B. (eds.) *Groupwork with Offenders.* London: Whiting and Birch.

Flood-Page, C. (1999). *The changing lives of young men.* Unpublished report for the Cabinet Office Social Exclusion Unit.

Flood-Page, C., Campbell, S., Harrington, V. and Miller, J. (2000). *Youth crime: Findings from the 1998/9 Youth Lifestyles Survey.* Home Office Research Study 209 London: Home Office.

Frances-Spence, M. (1995). 'Justice: Do they mean for us? Black Probation Officers and Black Clients in the Probation Service.' In Ward, D. and Lacey M. (eds.) *Probation: working for justice.* London: Whiting and Birch.

Graham, J. and Bowling, B. (1995). *Young people and crime* Home Office Research Study 145. London: Home Office.

Green, R. (1989). 'Probation and the black offender'. *New Community.* 16(1): 81-91.

HMIP. (2000). *Thematic Inspection Report: Towards Race Equality.* London: Home Office.

Home Office. (2001). *Probation Statistics England and Wales 1999.* London: Home Office.

Home Office. (2000). *Probation Statistics England and Wales 1998.* London: Home Office.

Inner London Probation Service. (1996). *Black and ethnic minority offenders experience of the Probation Service: June 1995.* London: ILPS.

Inner London Probation Service. (1993). *Working with difference: a positive and practical guide to anti-discriminatory practice teaching.* London: Inner London Probation Service.

Kett, J., Collett, S., Barron, C., Hill, I. and Metherell, D. (1991). *Managing and developing anti-racist practice within probation: a resource pack for action.* Merseyside: Merseyside Probation Service.

Lawrence, D. (1995). 'Race, Culture and the Probation Service' In McIvor, G. (ed.) *Working with Offenders.* London: Jessica Kingsley Publishers.

Mistry, T. (1993). 'Establishing a Feminist Model of Groupwork in the Probation Service' In Brown, A. and Caddick, B. (eds.) *Groupwork with Offenders.* London: Whiting and Birch.

NACRO. (1991). *Black Communities and the Probation Service: Working together for change.* A Report of the Sub-committee of the NACRO Race Issues Advisory Committee. London: NACRO.

NAPO. (1988). *Racism, representation and the criminal justice system.* London: NAPO.

National Probation Service – Thames Valley Research and Evaluation Unit. (2001). *Think First Inspection – Links with Case Management.* Unpublished report.

Pathak, S. (2000). *Race Research for the Future. Ethnicity in Education, Training and the Labour Market.* Research Topic Paper. London: DfEE.

Phillips, C., Considine, H. and Lewis, R. (2000). *A review of audits and strategies produced by crime and disorder partnerships in 1999.* Home Office briefing note 8/00. London: Home Office.

Raynor, P., Smith, D. and Vanstone, M. (1994). *Effective Probation Practice.* London: Macmillan.

Senior, P. (1993). 'Groupwork in the Probation Service: Care or Control in the 1990s' In Brown, A. and Caddick, B. (eds.) *Groupwork with Offenders.* London: Whiting and Birch.

Sly, F., Thair, T. and Risdon, A. (1999). 'Trends in the labour market participation of ethnic groups'. *Labour Market Trends. December 1999.* 631-639.

Smith, D.J. (1997). 'Ethnic Origins, Crime and Criminal Justice.' In Maguire, M. *et al.* (eds.) *The Oxford Handbook of Criminology.* Oxford: Clarendon Press.

Taylor, W. (1981). *Probation and after-care in a multi-racial society.* London: Commission for Racial Equality.

Tuklo Orenda Associates. (1999). *Making a Difference: A Positive and Practical Guide to Working with Black Offenders.* Written by Tuklo Orenda Associates for South West Probation Training Consortium, 1999. With support from the Home Office Probation Unit.

Vennard, J. and Hedderman, C. (1998). Effective interventions with offenders. In Goldblatt, P. and Lewis, C. (Eds.) *Reducing offending: an assessment of research evidence on ways of dealing with offending behaviour.* Home Office Research Study 187. London: Home Office.

Vennard, J., Sugg, D. and Hedderman, C. (1997). *Changing offenders' attitudes and behaviour: what works?* London: Home Office.

Williams, P. (2001). *Evaluation of the Black Offender Groupwork Programme.* Greater Manchester Probation Service.

RDS Publications

Requests for Publications

Copies of our publications and a list of those currently available may be obtained from:

> Home Office
> Research, Development and Statistics Directorate
> Communication Development Unit
> Room 275, Home Office
> 50 Queen Anne's Gate
> London SW1H 9AT
> Telephone: 020 7273 2084 (answerphone outside of office hours)
> Facsimile: 020 7222 0211
> E-mail: publications.rds@homeoffice.gsi.gov.uk

alternatively

why not visit the RDS web-site at
> Internet: http://www.homeoffice.gov.uk/rds/index.htm

where many of our publications are available to be read on screen or downloaded for printing.